A NOVEL BY JOHN BRILEY

Cry Freedom

Simplified by
Rowena Akinyemi

OXFORD UNIVERSITY PRESS

OXFORD
UNIVERSITY PRESS

Great Clarendon Street, Oxford OX2 6DP

Oxford University Press is a department of the University of Oxford.
It furthers the University's objective of excellence in research, scholarship,
and education by publishing worldwide in

Oxford New York

Auckland Cape Town Dar es Salaam Hong Kong Karachi
Kuala Lumpur Madrid Melbourne Mexico City Nairobi
New Delhi Shanghai Taipei Toronto

With offices in

Argentina Austria Brazil Chile Czech Republic France Greece
Guatemala Hungary Italy Japan Poland Portugal Singapore
South Korea Switzerland Thailand Turkey Ukraine Vietnam

OXFORD and OXFORD ENGLISH are registered trade marks of
Oxford University Press in the UK and in certain other countries

ISBN 978 0 19 479256 1

Printed in China

ACKNOWLEDGEMENTS

Photographs in this book are taken from the motion picture *Cry Freedom*,
starring Denzel Washington, and appear courtesy of Universal Studios Licensing LLLP,
© 1987 University City Studios, Inc. All rights reserved
Map by: Martin Ursell

Word count (main text): 29,420 words

Distributed By:
Grass Roots Press
Toll Free: 1-888-303-3213
Fax: (780) 413-6582
Web Site: www.grassrootsbooks.net

CRY FREEDOM

Up until 1994, when the first black government was elected, South Africa was both a beautiful country, and an ugly country. It was – indeed, still is – rich in gold and diamonds, but it was also a poor country, where people were forced to live together in small, dirty houses. It was a country of black people, with a government of white people. It was a country of contradictions.

Steve Biko was a black political leader who wanted to bring together the black and white people of South Africa. Donald Woods was the white editor of an important newspaper, and he wanted to help Biko. They were both good men, men with a vision of the future. But South Africa chose to silence them by banning them – and worse.

This book, and the film on which it was based, were created in order to inform the world about what was happening in South Africa in those years.

OXFORD BOOKWORMS LIBRARY

True Stories

Cry Freedom
Stage 6 (2500 headwords)

Series Editor: Jennifer Bassett
Founder Editor: Tricia Hedge
Activities Editors: Jennifer Bassett and Alison Baxter

CONTENTS

The Beginning

1

Where the River Buffalo flows into the warm Indian Ocean, on the south-east coast of South Africa, lies the city of East London, with its wonderful climate, beautiful sandy beaches, clear sea, and evergreen trees. It is the home, too, of the *Daily Dispatch*, the respected newspaper which in November 1975 began a new battle with the South African Government.

Donald Woods, editor of the *Daily Dispatch*, sat at his desk looking at the stories for the front page of tomorrow's newspaper. There was a story on the government's refusal of a new appeal for the release of Nelson Mandela. There was also a story on the pardon for Richard Nixon by President Ford of the United States of America, which Woods had intended to use as the main story. But news had just come in of a police raid on the black township called Crossroads, in Cape Town, more than a thousand kilometres away on the south-west tip of South Africa. Woods moved the stories around on his desk. He would make the Crossroads story the main story, and move news of a Japanese factory in Durban to the back page.

'Boss!' Ken Robertson, one of the journalists on the *Daily Dispatch*, burst into the office and threw a bundle of photographs on to Woods' desk. He lit a cigarette and began to smoke as Woods looked through the photographs.

They were pictures of the police raid on Crossroads: a woman holding a baby in her arms in front of her wrecked home; two policemen beating a boy; an old man sitting in an armchair, with broken walls around him; a policeman with a whip chasing a girl; a bulldozer smashing through a tiny kitchen.

Woods looked up at Ken in amazement. 'How did you get these?'

Ken smiled. 'I got them. Do we dare use them?'

Woods examined the pictures again. In Cape Town black workers could get work without work permits. Some of these workers brought their families with them, which was also against the law, and built a room for them out of wooden boxes or bits of tin. White employers benefited from the low wages the illegal workers accepted. However, from time to time, so that the town did not become permanent, the police came with whips and burning tear gas, forcing the men into police buses and moving them out of the city. Then the bulldozers came to tear apart the houses made of wooden boxes, and bits of tin.

Woods suddenly smiled. 'I'll print them,' he said. 'I'll even put your name underneath them.'

'Thanks!' Ken responded. 'If the police pick me up, your name will be the first on my lips!'

The law did not allow newspapers to print photographs of police beating black people, but if there were enough violent pictures the government sometimes let the matter drop in order to prevent the newspapers giving the public more information.

'Come on, tell me. How did you get these?' Woods demanded once more, staring at Ken through his glasses. His thick grey hair made him look older than his forty-two years.

'The newspaper will have to pay my expenses, that's all I can say about it. Drinking is the hardest part of my job!' Ken picked up one of the photographs. It showed a wall, covered with large pictures of the serious, handsome face of a young black man, with the name BIKO underneath. 'What about Mr Biko?' Ken asked. 'Will you use his name?'

'Was Mr Biko meeting his supporters in Crossroads?'

'I think so. I was told that his name was everywhere.'

Woods sat back in his chair and took off his glasses for a moment. 'No. Leave him out of the story. I want to write about him and his Black Consciousness in an editorial.'

Ken nodded and left the room with the pictures. Woods turned back to his desk. Woods did not believe that black people should be allowed to vote. He accepted the laws that forced blacks and whites to live in separate areas. But he had been trained as a lawyer, and he did not like police brutality against black people. He would put one of Ken's pictures at the top in the centre of the front page.

News had just come in of a police raid on Crossroads.

Newspapers all over South Africa used Ken's pictures of the raid on Crossroads. Woods received lots of phone calls – threats from the police, unknown callers making threats on his life, occasional words of congratulations from editors of other newspapers. The editorial attacking Stephen Biko, however, won approval from everyone. Or so Woods thought.

Mamphela Ramphele marched confidently into the offices of the *Daily Dispatch*. She was dressed in jeans and a white shirt and she looked beautiful. When she came to the receptionist's desk, she threw a newspaper down in front of Ann Hobart.

'I would like to know who's responsible for this,' she demanded.

Ann looked at the paper. It was folded to show Woods' editorial on Biko: BANTU STEPHEN BIKO – THE UGLY THREAT OF BLACK RACISM.

'*Doctor* Mamphela Ramphele,' she said, showing Ann her card. 'And I won't leave until he sees me.'

Ann hesitated. She was annoyed by this black woman who had so much confidence. But she picked up the phone. 'There's a Dr Ramphele wishing to speak to you, Mr Woods,' she said coldly.

Woods assumed that Dr Ramphele was an old man with some story to tell. 'Please send him in,' he answered.

Woods glanced up from his work as Ann opened the door and announced Dr Ramphele, and was amazed to see an angry young woman marching towards him.

Mamphela put the editorial on the desk in front of Woods. 'I've been reading this paper long enough to know that you're not one of the worst white journalists. So I'm surprised to think you would write such rubbish!'

Woods recovered from his surprise. 'Well, Dr Ramphele, I've written against white prejudice, and if you think I'm going to ignore black prejudice, then you're complaining to the wrong man!'

'Black prejudice!' Mamphela exploded in anger. 'That's not what Steve Biko believes in at all! Don't you find out the facts first, before you print?'

'I think I do understand what Mr Biko believes in!' Woods began angrily.

'Well, you understand wrong!' Mamphela interrupted. 'And he can't come to you, since he is banned. If you want to find out the truth, you ought to go and see him!'

Woods looked at Mamphela in silence. She was beautiful, intelligent, and full of confidence. 'Where are you from?' he asked at last, the anger gone from his voice.

'From here. From South Africa.' Mamphela was still angry. 'I was one of two from my tribal area to be given a place at Natal Medical School. I am an example of your white concern for the black people of this land.'

Woods almost lost his temper. Then he sighed, sat back in his chair, and threw his pencil down on the desk. 'Well,' he said slowly, 'I'm glad we didn't waste our money.'

Mamphela smiled slightly, the humour dissolving her anger. She moved away from the desk and sat down, staring at Woods as if wondering what to say next. At last she spoke again. 'I know you're not a fool, Mr Woods, but you *are* uninformed. Steve Biko is one of the few people who can still save South Africa. He's in King William's Town – that's his banning area. You ought to see him.'

Woods thought that her quiet sincerity was as impressive as her previous anger.

2

The road out of East London to the north gradually rises from the coast to grassy hills, and then descends again to the valley of the Buffalo River, about sixty kilometres from East London. Only whites live in King William's Town itself, of course. Woods, in his white Mercedes, drove through the black township, a few kilometres from the centre of the town, on his way to the address Dr Ramphele had given him. The houses were small and miserable, but the surrounding hills, covered with acacia trees, were beautiful.

Woods drove on, surprised that he was meeting a banned person at an address in the white town. He found the quiet, wide street with trees on both sides. The address was an old church, with small trees around it, and bits of broken fence. Woods parked across the street and stared at it for a moment. He noticed two security policemen under a tree not far away. They were obviously Biko's 'minders' and Woods smiled and waved at them. Biko needed watching, Woods believed, because he aimed to create separate black organizations, which Woods thought dangerous.

Woods got out of the car and walked across the street to the church door. He rang the rusty bell and immediately the door opened.

A young black woman, rather fat, greeted him with a warm smile. 'Mr Woods?'

'Yes. I'm here to see Steve Biko,' Woods said.

A little boy ran to her side, holding on to her skirt and staring shyly at the white man. 'I'm Steve's wife, Ntsiki,' she said, and opened the door wide.

Woods was surprised. Ntsiki was warm and friendly, not the sort of person he expected. He stepped inside the church and received another surprise. Some men and women were painting the walls while others were putting up partitions. Some girls were sewing in one corner of the church; there was a library of old books and magazines in another area; two older men were making children's toys in a third area.

'We're trying to create a centre where black people can meet during the day; maybe learn something, get information about jobs,' Ntsiki said as they walked through the church. The little boy, still holding his mother's skirt, smiled at Woods.

'And who is this one?' Woods asked, smiling down at the boy.

'Oh, this is Nkosinathi. He's sometimes more trouble than his father,' Ntsiki said. She opened a side door, smiling again. 'He's waiting for you, Mr Woods.'

Woods stepped through the door, and the door shut immediately behind him. He looked around, but could see no one. He was in the church yard, untidy with long grass. There was a huge old tree in the centre whose long, green branches touched the ground, the sun shining through the leaves. There was silence, except for the wind blowing through the leaves of the tree.

Woods walked forwards, looking for someone. There was a small building at the other side of the yard, but there was no sign of anyone. Woods began to feel annoyed. Then something near the tree caught his eye. A tall black figure was standing quite still, watching Woods.

'Biko? Are you Steve Biko?' Woods called out.

The person turned away, moving towards the small building. 'Come, follow me.'

Woods felt even more annoyed. He sighed and walked across the yard to the building. He looked through the open door and saw that it was a small office. The man stood in the shadows behind the desk and Woods could not see enough of the face to recognize whether the man was Biko or not. The man's large, dark eyes watched Woods in silence.

'May I come in?' Woods finally asked.

The person nodded.

Woods sighed again and stepped into the office. 'I don't have all day to play games, and I . . .'

'I would have met you in the church, but as you know I can be with only one person at a time. The System are just across the street.'

Now that they were face to face Woods could see that this man was Biko. He was young and handsome; his deep, dark eyes were alive and sensitive. Woods knew that 'System' was the word blacks used for any white authority – police, government, army – and that Biko was referring to the two security policemen in the street.

'Of course, you approve of my banning,' Biko went on.

Woods was tempted to say: 'You're right!' But he hesitated; he had come to hear Biko's opinions. 'I think your ideas are dangerous; but no, I don't approve of banning,' he said finally.

'A true "liberal"!' Biko declared.

'I'm not ashamed of being a liberal,' Woods responded sharply. 'You disapprove of liberals, I understand.'

Biko smiled. 'Disapproval is too strong a word,' he protested. 'I just think that a white liberal, who holds on to the advantages of his white world – jobs, houses, education, Mercedes – is perhaps not the right person to tell blacks how they should react to the way this country is governed.'

Woods nodded coolly. 'I wonder what kind of liberal *you* would make, Mr Biko, if you were the one who possessed the house, the job, the Mercedes – and the whites lived in the townships.'

Biko laughed aloud. 'Now that is a charming idea. Whites in the townships and me in a Mercedes.' Then he smiled, warm and sincere as his wife, and put out his hand. 'It was good of you to come, Mr Woods. I've wanted to meet you for a long time.'

Woods hesitated for a moment, observing the quick change in mood, the intelligence, the unexpected sincerity in the eyes and the warmth of the smile. Then he put out his own hand and took Biko's.

It was the beginning.

Education of a Liberal

3

Later that morning Donald Woods and Steve Biko drove out to Zanempilo, where Biko had started a clinic. Zanempilo was about twenty-five kilometres from King William's Town, in hill country so dry that there were no farms in sight. Biko's 'minders' – the two security policemen – followed in their own car.

Woods glanced at them in the mirror. 'They follow you everywhere?' he asked.

Biko smiled. He put his arm out of the window and waved at the car behind. 'They think they do.'

The clinic at Zanempilo was at the top of a hill. The first thing Woods noticed was the church. In addition, there were three long, low buildings made of wood. A line of people queued outside one of the buildings – women with small children, old men, pregnant women.

Woods parked his car. The police waited further back on the road. 'So this is it?' Woods asked, getting out of the car.

'This is it,' Biko replied. 'A clinic for black people, with black workers, and a black doctor.'

Mamphela came out of the door of one of the buildings. She was in a doctor's white coat, some papers in her hand. She paused and stared at Woods and Biko. Then she nodded at them and turned to her patients.

'Was this place her idea or yours?' Woods challenged, looking at Biko across the top of the car.

'It was an idea that came from all of us,' Biko replied. He looked at Mamphela. 'But we were lucky to get her,' he added.

The clinic was an amazing achievement, anyway, Woods thought. He knew that Biko's Black Consciousness group wanted black people to create their own organizations. But Woods himself believed that South Africa needed organizations where black and white people could work together.

'So if you had a white "liberal" doctor working here, that wouldn't serve your purpose?' Woods asked.

Biko became more serious than Woods had yet heard him.

'When I was a student, I suddenly realized that it wasn't just the job I was studying for that was white. The history we read was made by white men, written by white men. Television, medicine, cars' – he hit the roof of the Mercedes – 'all invented by white men. Even football.' He paused for a moment. 'In a world like that, it is hard not to believe that there is something inadequate about being born black.' He stopped again and then glanced behind him at the two policemen watching him from a distance. 'I began to think that this feeling was a bigger problem than the things the System does to us.' Slowly he turned back to Woods. 'I felt that, first, the black man has to believe he has the same ability to be a doctor – a leader – as a white man.'

Woods nodded. He understood Biko's ideas and he was impressed by the man who had them.

Biko looked at the clinic. 'So we started this clinic. My mistake was to write down some of my ideas.'

'And the government banned you.'

Biko nodded. 'And the white liberal editor started attacking me.'

'I attacked you for your racism, for refusing to work with white liberals,' Woods protested.

Biko smiled. 'How old are you, Mr Woods?' he enquired.

Woods hesitated, a little annoyed by the question. 'Forty-two,' he answered. 'If that makes any difference.'

Biko stared at him. 'A white South African,' he said slowly. 'A newspaper man, forty-two years old. Have you spent any time in a black township?'

Woods hesitated again. He had driven through a few townships, but no white South African spent any time in one. 'I've . . . I've been to many . . .'

Biko smiled. 'Don't be embarrassed. Apart from the police, I don't suppose one white South African in ten thousand has spent any time in a black township.' Biko stopped smiling at Woods' embarrassment and his voice grew warm, as if he were speaking to an old friend. 'You see, we know how *you* live. We cook your food, clear your rubbish, cut your grass,' he said quietly. 'Would you like to see how *we* live, the ninety per cent of South Africans who are forced to leave your white streets at six o'clock at night?'

It was not an empty challenge: Biko meant it.

Later that afternoon Woods went home to his swimming pool. Four of his five children were at home, and the three boys – Duncan, Dillon, and Gavin – splashed about with him. Mary, aged five and the youngest of the family, was playing at the side of the pool. Charlie, their big dog, ran up and down, excited by all the noise. At last Woods swam to the edge, the boys chasing him and splashing water at him. Woods got out of the pool and ran quickly to the shower which was in the garden near the pool.

'I'm going to write to your teacher and tell him to give you more work,' Woods shouted to the boys as he turned on the shower.

As he came out of the shower, his wife, Wendy, arrived home with Jane, their eldest child, aged fourteen. Wendy left the shopping in the car and came down the garden to greet Woods.

'Well? What was he like?' Wendy asked, as Charlie jumped up at her.

Woods rubbed his hair with a towel. 'Well, he's like his photographs: young, tall, handsome.'

'Donald! I mean what kind of person is he?' Wendy was more liberal politically than Donald, but she did not agree with Black Consciousness.

Woods sat down. 'I'm not sure. They've built a clinic up there in Zanempilo. Everyone working there is black. You should see it. People come from miles.'

Wendy stared at him doubtfully. 'Where did they get the money?'

'From churches, abroad. From black people. Even some companies gave them some money.'

Amazed, Wendy asked, 'South African companies?'

'That's right,' Woods answered. 'Surprisingly, someone important heard Biko make a speech and was impressed. I must tell you, he is impressive.'

Evalina, their black servant, brought a glass of orange juice for Wendy and put it down on the table. Then she went up the garden to the car, to get the shopping.

'He hasn't convinced you that Black Consciousness is right, has he?' Wendy asked.

Woods hesitated. 'No. But I *have* agreed to visit a black township with him.'

Wendy was silent, wondering how Biko had persuaded her husband to do this. 'But he's banned,' she said finally. 'How can he go anywhere with you?'

Woods shook his head, smiling at Wendy's amazed face. Then he leaned forward and kissed her. 'I'm not sure. But I intend to find out.'

4

Biko put on the old brown army coat that all black workers wore, and then pulled on an old hat. Tonight, three weeks after their first meeting, he was going with Woods to a black township outside East London.

'It's not worth the risk, is it, Steve?' Mamphela asked.

Biko smiled. 'The education of a white liberal? It is a duty.'

Mamphela was not amused. 'If you get caught outside your banning area, *you* go to prison. Mr Woods would only have to write a letter of explanation to the Board of his newspaper.'

'That's what we call justice in South Africa, didn't you know?' Biko replied.

Mamphela smiled at that and sat down at the typewriter. She was working in Biko's office on a speech she was going to give. 'I don't want them to get you in prison again,' she said.

'We won't get caught,' Biko said confidently. 'When I put the light on, someone must sit at my desk and read until I get back, that's all.'

Woods had put on some old clothes for the visit to the black township. He drove out of East London and parked his car in a small country road, about four kilometres from town. There he waited. A few minutes later a black taxi drove up and stopped beside him. The door opened.

'Get in, man!' Mapetla said urgently, and pushed Woods into the back seat. This was not easy, because there were already three black men sitting in it. Mapetla got in after him and banged the door shut.

The car drove away fast, and John Qumza, who was driving, looked in the mirror anxiously. 'Get him down in the middle! We don't want him sitting up there where no one can miss seeing him!'

Roughly, Mapetla pulled Woods down until he was squashed underneath two of the men. Woods had already met Mapetla Mohapi, who worked at the clinic in Zanempilo.

'You said you were going to wear old clothes,' Mapetla said angrily.

'But I am!' Woods protested.

'Give him your hat, Dyani,' Mapetla ordered one of the other men.

Dyani removed the dirty hat from his head and Mapetla pushed it on to Woods' grey hair.

'Pull it all the way down at the back!' John shouted from the driver's seat. John Qumza had first met Biko at university and was one of the leaders of the black student organization which Biko led.

Mapetla pulled the hat down at the back of Woods' head.

Woods was so squashed that he could not move his hands to adjust the hat himself. 'You might just push the hair out of my eyes, too,' he asked, and Mapetla smiled for the first time.

The car was a black taxi. The law said that some taxis were for blacks and some for whites only. Black taxis were usually very old cars and usually carried as many passengers as could be squashed in them. John turned down another small road and Biko stepped out from behind some small acacia trees. He got into the front seat, and one of the men already in the front seat sat on his knees. There were now four men in the front seat and five in the back.

Biko turned round and glanced at Woods. 'You comfortable enough?'

Everyone laughed. 'Hell, he's got the best seat,' Mapetla declared.

'Listen, I'm quite comfortable,' Woods said, in his own defence. 'I was brought up in a black Homeland, you know.'

'I know,' Biko responded. 'You only drive that Mercedes because of the neighbours. A white liberal like you really wants to ride in buses and taxis like us.'

Everyone laughed again. There was an atmosphere of fun and adventure in the taxi as the men joked with each other. But as the taxi reached the black township outside East London, and moved slowly in a long, dusty line of buses and taxis, the mood changed. They were all silent as they stared out at the crowds of people walking through the little streets. As Woods looked at all those black faces, tired and unsmiling, he felt that the whole black world, which he had believed he knew so well, had a life he was totally unaware of. It was getting dark now, and they drove through the streets until most of them were empty and the evening rush was over.

'Let's stretch our legs,' Biko said at last. John stopped the car and they all got out stiffly, bending and stretching their arms and legs.

Finally, Biko stood up and looked at Woods, his eyes searching his face. Then he smiled tightly. 'Let's take a walk.'

He led Woods off the main street, down a little side path. John and Mapetla walked behind them, guarding them. They moved along between the little houses, some with electric lights, others with oil lamps. Smoke from wood fires hung over the whole area. Several old men were cooking over fires outside. Women carried buckets of water from taps on the street. Men stood at their doors, watching the street. Twice they saw gangs of black youths walking the streets, looking for trouble. It was a new world to Woods.

They turned a corner and saw a little boy looking out of the door of one of the houses. He checked the street for danger – looking at Woods and Biko – and then ran as fast as he could to another house down the street.

Biko spoke for the first time. 'Run, son, run,' he said quietly, as they watched the boy go. He turned to Woods. 'Most of the women here work as domestic servants, so they see their children for a couple of hours on Sundays, that's all. This place is full of violence. I'm amazed that children survive here at all.'

'Were you brought up in a township?' Woods enquired.

'Mostly. My father died when I was seventeen and I went away for two years to a school where I was taught by German and Swiss priests. But if you do survive in a township and you get the education the white man gives you, then you go to work in their city – you see their houses, their streets, their cars. And you begin to feel there is something not quite right about you. Something to do with your blackness. Because no matter how stupid or how clever a white child is, he is born into his white world. But you, the black child, clever or stupid, are born into this . . . and, clever or stupid, you will die in it . . .'

Biko's eyes turned to Woods. Woods did not try to respond to Biko's words and they walked on silently. Then Biko spoke again. 'And even to stay in a legal township like this one, the white boss must sign your pass every month, the white government tells you which house to live in and what the rent is. You can never own land or pass anything on to your children. The land belongs to the white man . . . and you, all you have got to give your children is this . . .' And Biko touched the black skin of his face.

Woods had never before understood the emptiness, the despair of the black community. Biko's words made him feel it that night, all around him, like something living.

5

'Come on,' Biko said a little later. 'I'm taking you to eat with a black family here.'

The little township house they went to was divided into four rooms. It was the home of Tenjy Mtintso, a tiny, pretty girl of twenty who worked as a nurse at the clinic in Zanempilo, and she was there to greet them. A big family lived in those four rooms: father, mother, son; aunt, uncle and three children; four other cousins.

The meal itself was a meat soup with rice and bread, served on big plates. There was no electricity in the house but two oil lamps hung from the ceiling. Biko served beer to everyone, smiling and putting his arms round Tenjy's aunt. It was a noisy and happy meal.

'You know, this feels like home to me,' Woods said. 'My father had a shop in a Homeland, and we were often the only white family for miles.' Woods wanted to impress them, but what he did not say was that in all those years he had never eaten with a black family.

'Homelands are not home to us, and the land is no good; that's why the government wants us to go and live there,' Mapetla declared.

After dinner the women washed the dishes, bringing water

from an outside tap and heating it on the cooker. Then, they began to wash their work clothes. The men sat and talked, some sitting in chairs, others on the floor.

'I'll tell you what happened when the white man first came to Africa,' Mapetla began. 'First, he says, "Do you mind if I pass through here?" "Hell, no, man," we say. "This land belongs to God." Then he comes back. "Do you mind if I bring my wife and children?" "Of course not," we say. "There's lots of land. We're just going to hunt over the hills for a couple of days." Then the white man finds a place he likes and builds a fence around it. "I'm going to have a farm here," he says. "OK," we say. "We'll just move round you, friend." Then the white man moves his fences outwards and says, "Look, when you go by you disturb my cattle. Don't come this way." We move off. But then the white man gets his gun and says, "Listen, we can't have people moving about all over the place like this. You must have a pass, so we know who is coming and going".'

Woods smiled, looking at Biko who was sitting on the floor near him. 'I'm not defending the past. But if you stopped listening to Steve Biko and let us liberals gradually fit you into our society, then . . .'

Tenjy put down the bucket of water she was carrying. 'Yes. You want to give us a *slightly* better education, so we can get *slightly* better jobs . . .'

'At first, maybe,' Woods said. 'But only at first. In the long . . .'

John interrupted. 'First or last. What you are saying is that your society is better than ours, so you liberals are going to teach us how to do things your way.'

'We don't want to be put into your society,' Biko said

forcefully. 'I am going to be me – as I am – and you can put me in prison, or even kill me, but I'm not going to be what *you* want me to be.'

There were no smiles now, and Woods felt the anger in the room. He tried to remain calm and reasonable. 'There are some advantages in our society: fewer white babies die, and we have more . . .'

'Guns and bombs and anxiety,' Biko interrupted. 'You can blow up the whole earth if one man makes a mistake. In your white society, when you knock on someone's door, if he is a nice person he will say, "What can I do for you?" He assumes that people are there to get something from him. But we don't think that way. We just say, "Come on in!" We like people. We don't think that life is an endless competition.'

Woods laughed, and Biko responded with a smile.

'You say you were brought up with blacks. Have you noticed that all our songs are group songs? – not someone singing to the moon about how lonely he is.'

Woods laughed again, and nodded.

Tenjy had finished washing her work clothes and now began to hang them above the cooker to dry for tomorrow. 'We know the great white powers have given the world industry and medicine,' she said, and paused to look at Woods. 'But maybe our society has something to give others, too, by teaching people how to live together. We don't want to lose that.'

'She's right,' Tenjy's uncle said. 'This is an African country. Let us have our place, in our own way, and then we will come together with our white brothers and sisters and find a way to live in peace. It cannot be just your way.'

'That sounds fair,' Woods admitted. 'But you can't go

back. The twentieth century is marching on for all of us.'

'But we want to march to our own time,' Mapetla declared bitterly. 'The best you want for us is to sit at *your* table with *your* knives and forks; and if we learn to do it right, you will kindly let us stay. We want to wipe the table clean. It is an *African* table. We are going to sit at it in our own right.'

Woods stared silently at Mapetla. He had never heard such bitterness before and he tried to accept Mapetla's anger.

John touched his hand. 'You will sit at that table, too. We know this is your home as it is our home. But you will not sit as the boss, but as one of the family.'

Woods sighed. 'I'm relieved that you are planning to allow us to sit at all!'

Everyone smiled at this remark and Tenjy's uncle poured more beer into Woods' glass. 'You understand our language,' he said; 'you know that the word we use for nephew is "my brother's son". Tenjy calls my wife not "aunt" but "mother's sister". We have no separate words for members of the family – all begin with "brother" and "sister". And we look after each other.'

Woods had learned the language as a boy and he knew that this was true. He realized now that it was perhaps a way of keeping the family together.

'In our traditional villages there were no starving men,' Mapetla added. 'The land belonged to everyone. No one slept on the streets, no children were abandoned.'

Tenjy stopped as she passed with some more clothes to wash. 'We got a lot of things right that your society has never solved.'

Woods smiled at her. 'You did have tribal wars, you know, in this perfect land of yours.'

'What do you call the First World War and the Second World War?' Biko asked.

There was a moment of silence and then they all laughed. 'You all put the words together well – but there's something about it that frightens me,' Woods said.

'Of course there is,' Mapetla responded. 'In your world everything white is normal – the way the world should be – and everything black is wrong, or some kind of mistake.'

'And your real achievement', Biko added, 'is that for years you've convinced most of us of that idea, too.'

Woods felt that this was not the whole truth. 'You're being unfair to a lot of people who . . .'

But Biko did not let him finish. 'In fact, our case is very simple,' he said quietly. 'We believe in an intelligent God. We believe that He knew what He was doing when He created the black man. Just as He did when He created the white man . . .'

Biko and Woods stared at each other. The quiet, serious words affected Woods more than anything he had seen that whole eventful day.

Confrontation

6

One morning six weeks later Donald Woods arrived late at the offices of the *Daily Dispatch*. Tenjy and Mapetla followed him. Woods knew that they were nervous as they entered this centre of white power and influence. People stopped to stare at them as they walked quickly through the newsroom. One journalist spilt coffee all over her desk and did not notice until the little procession had entered Woods' office.

Ken Robertson was sitting on the edge of Woods' desk, reading, when Woods came in. He lifted his head to speak – but stopped with his mouth open.

Woods hung his jacket on the back of his chair. 'Ken, this is Tenjy Mtintso and Mapetla Mohapi,' he said. 'They are from King William's Town, and I'm glad to say that the Board has approved their appointment here.'

Ken stared at Woods. Then he stared at Tenjy and Mapetla. There was no doubt: they were black. Ken had heard that yesterday's meeting of the Board had been noisy, but he had not guessed this!

Woods picked up the phone. 'Ann, please come and meet two new reporters.' He turned to Ken. 'When they've had a look around the office, I want you to teach them how to use our cameras.'

Ken nodded, still unable to speak. Ann came in.

'Ann, this is Tenjy and Mapetla. Please show them around the office.'

'Of course,' Ann murmured. She looked at Woods for some further explanation, but Woods began looking at the letters on his desk and said nothing more. Ann turned and went out of the room with Tenjy and Mapetla. Ken did not leave.

'Excuse me, boss,' he began. 'Ah . . . where will they be working?'

Woods looked up and waved his hand towards the large open office area beyond the glass walls of his own office. 'In the newsroom.'

Ken nodded. 'The newsroom. Of course. Who would have

thought of anything else? Tell me, does this Steve Biko practise black magic?'

Woods smiled. 'They're going to cover black news – weddings, music, sport, crime. There is nothing illegal in that, and we'll get a lot of new readers.'

'Oh, I'm sure the white readers will be delighted! And when they start writing about Black Consciousness –' he raised both hands – 'great news!'

In fact, it was Biko's idea that Woods should use a black journalist. Wendy – who had visited the clinic at Zanempilo and who had become friends with Mamphela, Ntsiki and Biko himself – thought that Woods should use a black woman. In the end, Woods convinced himself that they needed both a black woman and a black man. And finally the Board had agreed.

Not long afterwards, Woods invited Ken to meet him out in the country one Sunday afternoon. They parked their cars off the road and five minutes later a black taxi appeared with Mapetla in the back seat.

'Where are we going?' Ken demanded. 'Should I have let my family know I might not be back?'

'You're going to a black football match,' Mapetla answered. 'The only danger is that you will lose your idea that whites play the best football in this country.'

In fact there was a whole world of black sport in South Africa, though no national teams because of the pass laws which prevented blacks from moving freely about the country.

When they arrived at the football field there were lots of people there already. As they walked towards the small stadium, three tall, tough men stepped in front of them, ready to prevent them from going in.

'Excuse me,' one said. 'Can I help you?'

Mapetla stepped forward. 'It's all right. They're friends of Steve Biko.'

The man stared. 'Biko? He's in King William's Town,' he said coldly. 'He's got nothing to do with this game.'

'Listen, man,' Mapetla protested, 'don't worry. These whites, they . . .'

John Qumza suddenly appeared, running towards them. 'They are OK!' he called. 'Steve asked them to come. Hello, Mr Woods.' He appealed again to the three men. 'Come on, if they were the System, they wouldn't be waiting for your permission.'

One of the men reached out and took Ken's camera. '*They* may be OK, but this certainly is not.'

'You're right,' John said quickly. 'Mapetla, please take the camera and put it in my car.' He gave Mapetla the keys and the tough men stood back to let the two white men pass into the stadium, though they still did not look very happy.

The two teams were already on the field, but the crowd was listening to a man with a microphone.

'Why does the white man stir up trouble between us?' the man asked the crowd. He was dressed in brown and gold, Mzimbi, a black leader who was wanted by the security police because he openly called for violent revolution. 'Because when we fight among ourselves, he can convince our friends overseas that it is right to tell us where to live, and how to live.'

John led Woods and Ken up the steps to some seats near the top of the stadium.

'He can go on paying us less for doing the same job as the white man. And he can go on passing his laws without listening to one word we say!' The crowd cheered angrily, some people standing up. 'We have got to keep together. Last year they killed more than four hundred black students! As one people we must let the white man know that his free ride on the back of black workers is over! If the only way we can get the message to him is to make sure he can never sleep in his big white bed in his big white house and know he is safe – then that is how it must be!'

The crowd shouted in support and Mzimbi raised his hands. Finally, Mzimbi made a sign that the crowd should be silent and people began to sit down. 'Now, we have got a surprise for you. He is a little shy – but you listen to what he has to say.' And then, waving, he turned and disappeared into the crowd, protected by a group of guards.

For a moment there was silence. Then another voice began to speak through another microphone. 'This is the biggest illegal meeting I have ever seen!'

The crowd burst into laughter. Woods recognized Biko's voice immediately, but he could not see him. He wondered anxiously how Biko would deal with the crowd since he did not agree with the call for violence.

'I heard what the last speaker said, and I agree – we are going to change South Africa! All we have to decide is the best way to do that. Believe me, the white man can be defeated!'

The crowd responded, and Woods stopped worrying. With humour and skill Biko had gained the approval of the crowd.

'We have the right to be angry,' Biko continued, 'but let us remember we are in this struggle not to kill *someone* but to kill the *idea* that one kind of man is better than another kind of man.'

'There!' Ken pointed to the right. Woods saw him – Biko at the back of the stadium with a microphone in his hand. John Qumza stood on his right, and Mapetla on his left, others surrounding them.

'Killing that idea does not depend on the white man. We must stop looking to the white man to *give* us anything. We have got to fill the black community with our own pride – not something the white man gives us, but something we make out of our own lives!'

The crowd was listening quietly now. Even the football players on the field were sitting on the ground, listening.

'We have got to teach our children black history,' Biko went on, 'tell them about our black heroes, our black society, so that they face the white man believing they are equal.'

And now the crowd did react, with loud, steady clapping.

'*Then*,' Biko declared forcefully, '*then* we will stand up to him in any way he chooses. Confrontation if he likes, but an open hand, too – to say that we can both build a South Africa worth living in. A South Africa for equal men – black or white. A South Africa as beautiful as this land is, as beautiful as we are!'

There was a second of silence and then the crowd responded – cheering, clapping, whistling – all rising to their feet. Woods stood and clapped with everyone else. Ken stared at him in amazement. Finally, he too stood up slowly and began to clap, joining the rest of the crowd.

7

Supporters of black revolution in South Africa say that if three black people meet together, one of them will be an informer for the government. There is some truth in this. There are so many ways to bribe informers: a job, a work permit for a son or daughter. It was not surprising, therefore, when not long after the football match Biko's 'minders' were told to bring Biko in to the police station in King William's Town.

The informer's great fear is of discovery and revenge, so the police hide informers in order to protect them. When the police brought Biko into Captain De Wet's office they held him in a chair in front of a large box, the kind used for a fridge. There was a hole in the box, and through the hole Biko saw a pair of eyes and part of a black face.

'That's him,' a voice said from within the box. 'That's the man who made the speech.'

Captain De Wet stepped in front of Biko and smiled down at him as the informer moved out of the back of the box and went out of the door. The two detectives stood behind Biko's chair.

'You know I don't call for violence, De Wet,' Biko said, 'but don't make the mistake of treating me without respect.'

'Out of your banning area, talking to a crowd,' De Wet said slowly, the smile no longer on his face. 'You're going to be in big trouble soon. You'll be up there in court facing all kinds of charges.'

Biko was unafraid. 'On what evidence? What's his name?' he nodded towards the box. 'Captain De Wet, you aren't going to send me to court in Pretoria on the evidence of an informer in a box, are you?' De Wet did not answer and Biko smiled. 'Everyone knows that an informer will say anything.'

De Wet paused and then bent his head to look straight into Biko's eyes. 'You are a bit of poison, Biko,' he said slowly. 'And I'm going to see you in prison.'

Biko smiled again. 'Not with that kind of evidence. Hell, we don't want you looking like a fool.'

In a flash of anger De Wet lifted his hand to hit Biko in the face. But Biko moved sideways fast, and the hand missed him.

'Don't!' Biko said, controlling his own anger.

The two detectives held Biko's arms and pulled him back tight against the chair. Biko continued to stare at De Wet, challenging him with the anger in his eyes. De Wet glanced at the two detectives and then quickly hit Biko across the face, knocking his head to one side and bringing blood to his mouth. Biko pulled his head back, the blood running down his chin, but his eyes were still fixed on De Wet. De Wet, satisfied that Biko understood who was boss in this building, nodded to the two detectives to release Biko's arms.

Instantly, Biko jumped up and hit De Wet across the face with similar force. De Wet almost fell, banging into the box, blood pouring from his nose. The two detectives were on Biko immediately, pushing him back across the room, one of them pulling out a short, heavy stick.

'No! Wait! No, man, don't beat him!' De Wet shouted in Afrikaans. It stopped the detectives. De Wet moved slowly back across the room, wiping the blood from his face. 'Remember, he's going to be a witness at another trial. We don't want him to look as if something happened to him.'

Finally De Wet came face to face with Biko. He studied him with cold hatred. 'You're lucky, Biko – lucky.'

Biko was still held firmly by the two detectives, but he did not respond to the hatred in De Wet's voice. 'I just expect to be treated in the same way as you expect to be treated,' he declared.

'Treated like a white man? You and your big ideas,' De Wet replied.

Biko smiled. 'If you're afraid of ideas, you'd better give in now.'

'We shall never give in,' De Wet growled.

The two detectives were holding Biko tighter and tighter but he remained smiling and struggled to speak. 'Come on,' he said, 'don't be afraid. Once you try, you'll see that there's nothing to be afraid of. We're just as weak and human as you are.'

For a second De Wet did not understand, but then the idea hit him. His face went red with anger. 'We're going to catch you one day, then we'll see how human you are.'

De Wet wanted the depth of hatred in that threat to be clearly understood by Biko. He wanted Biko to live with that threat, to live with that promise of revenge every day and

Biko stared at De Wet, challenging him with the anger in his eyes.

every night of his life. When he felt Biko understood, he nodded to the two detectives.

'Throw him out,' he said. And the two detectives pulled Biko from the chair, through the police station, and threw him out of the side door into the street.

It was a quite different Steve Biko who entered the witness box two weeks later in a court in Pretoria, the capital of South Africa, eight hundred kilometres north of King William's Town. He was dressed in a suit, a tie, a white shirt. As he put his hand out to swear on the Bible, he stood tall and proud, the physical equal of anyone in the court. His intelligence was going to be tested by the State Prosecutor and Judge Regter.

Two years earlier two students' organizations had arranged a large meeting in support of the new government in Mozambique. The South African Government banned the meeting and arrested a group of Black Consciousness leaders who were helping to organize it. For a long time they were kept in prison without being charged, but at last charges were brought against them and Biko – who was involved with both the students' organizations – was called as the main witness for the defence.

The State Prosecutor began. 'This student organization declares that "South Africa is a country in which both black and white shall live together". What does that mean?'

Biko did not hesitate. 'It means that we believe South Africa needs all parts of the community.'

The Prosecutor was a little surprised by Biko's quick response. 'I see. Are you familiar with the language of some of the documents which the defendants have discussed with black groups?'

'Yes, since I wrote some of the documents.'

'Ah, you did? The one which noted the terrorism of the government?'

'Correct.'

This short answer surprised the Prosecutor even further. Wendy – who had come to Pretoria for the trial and was sitting in the white area of the court – glanced across at Ntsiki and Mamphela, sitting in the black area of the court, and they exchanged an anxious smile.

'You say "terrorism". Do you honestly believe that?' the Prosecutor asked.

'I do,' Biko answered. 'I am not talking about *words*, I am talking about violence – about police beating people, about police shooting people. I am talking about people starving in the townships. I am talking about desperate, hopeless people. I think all that amounts to more terrorism than the words the defendants have spoken. But they stand charged in this court and white society is not charged.'

The court was silent. Then the Prosecutor spoke again. 'So your answer to this is to encourage violence in the black community?'

'No. We want to avoid violence.'

The Prosecutor was convinced that Biko was now trapped. 'You write here that your true leaders are in prison in Robben Island, or forced to live overseas. Who are these true leaders?'

'I mean men like Nelson Mandela, Robert Sobukwe, Govan Mbeki.'

The Prosecutor looked at Biko with a smile. 'Is it not true that all these men call for black violence?'

'All these men are willing to struggle and fight against the situation of black people in this country,' Biko responded, and there was a murmur of agreement from the black area of the court. The Judge frowned in that direction.

'So you agree with these men?' the Prosecutor continued.

'I agree with their concern. Their sacrifices for black people have given them the natural support of all of us. Even if we do not agree with some of the things they did, they spoke the language of the people, and they will always have a place in our hearts.'

Again, there was a murmur of agreement from the black area of the court, and again Judge Regter turned and frowned.

'And you do not agree with their call for violence?' asked the Prosecutor.

'We believe that we can progress without violence.'

'But your own words call for direct confrontation!'

'That is right. We will not accept society as it exists in South Africa. We demand confrontation.'

The Prosecutor stared at Biko in amazement. Surely he was trapped now! 'In other words, you demand violence?'

'No,' Biko replied calmly. 'You and I are now in confrontation, but I see no violence.'

There was some laughter, but the Prosecutor was silent. Judge Regter leaned forward. 'But nowhere in these documents do you say that the white government is doing any good.'

Biko turned to Judge Regter. 'It does so little good that it is not worth writing about.'

This time the laughter was louder, and Judge Regter glanced round the court. 'But you still think that you can influence the government without violence?'

'Yes, sir.' Biko spoke with respect. It was obvious that Judge Regter was trying to conduct a fair trial. 'I believe that this government will listen to black opinion. Prime Minister Vorster can postpone some problems, but as black voices grow louder, he will be forced to listen; he is going to consider the feelings of black people.'

Judge Regter was still trying to understand. 'But if you accuse the government of terrorism, surely you encourage black violence?'

For the first time Biko hesitated. He wanted Judge Regter, and the whole court, and the journalists who were present, to understand what he was going to say. 'Black people are aware of the things they suffer. They don't need us to tell them what the government is doing to them.' There was some laughter, and Biko smiled. But his face quickly became serious again. 'We are telling them to stop accepting those problems, to confront them. Black society has lost hope in itself, it feels defeated. We believe that black people must not give in; they must find ways – even in this situation – to develop hope.

'Black people must not give in; they must find ways to develop hope.'

Hope for themselves, hope for this country. That is the whole point of Black Consciousness – to build within ourselves a sense of our own humanity, our proper place in the world . . .'

The whole court was silent, filled with Biko's own humanity. What had begun as an attack on Black Consciousness had become a platform for Biko's views, for the power and sincerity of his words. The next day, all South African. newspapers printed news of the trial. Woods printed Biko's words in full.

8

The next Board meeting was not easy for Woods. Biko was a banned person and it was against the law to print his words. The trial was different, Woods argued, since it *was* legal to print words used in court. Many newspapers had used Biko's words, so Woods was sure that the government would not attack one particular newspaper. In spite of this, the Board still felt that Woods was putting the newspaper in a dangerous position.

However, there was no doubt that black news and black readers were now accepted by everyone. Tenjy wrote an article on the community centre in King William's Town, which brought in a flood of gifts from both black and white people.

Biko phoned Woods to thank him. 'It's amazing what one positive article can do.'

'Be careful,' Woods joked. 'You'll be talking like a liberal soon!'

'Oh, no,' Biko laughed. 'It's going to take more than a few pots and pans and a second-hand fridge to do that!'

That night, Dilima, the elderly man who was the night guard at the old church in King William's Town, was disturbed by noises outside in the yard. He was sleeping in the sewing room, but he sat up and listened. Someone was trying to force open the front door. Boys, perhaps, who had heard about all the gifts.

Suddenly the front door crashed open and Dilima saw three big men, with hoods covering their heads and faces, and carrying iron bars. Another man, also wearing a hood, followed and gave an order in Afrikaans. Then they began to smash everything – windows, typewriters, chairs, children's toys.

Shaking with fear, Dilima quietly moved towards the side door. He slipped outside and closed the door softly behind him. He wanted to get to Biko's office to use the telephone, but as he moved towards it he saw three other men in that room, too. Dilima ran for the tree in the middle of the yard and quietly pulled himself up on the first branch. As he watched, he saw one of the men pull the telephone in Biko's room from the wall and smash it on the desk.

At last, two of the men came out, breathing heavily, and stopped under the tree. The third man joined them, and spoke in Afrikaans, ordering them to help the men in the church. Then he pulled the hood from his head. Dilima recognized him immediately. It was Captain De Wet from the security police.

The next day Biko asked Woods to come to the church with Wendy. It was a terrible sight. Everything of value had been smashed. Wendy began to help Ntsiki and Mamphela clear the wreckage.

'Who do you go to when the police attack you?' Ntsiki asked sadly, not expecting an answer.

But Wendy stopped and looked across at Woods. 'Donald, go to Kruger. He's the Minister of Police and he told you himself that he wants to fight police illegality. Well, go and tell him.'

Mamphela was picking up papers from the floor. She laughed at Wendy's suggestion. 'Kruger? He would probably give them a reward!'

Woods lit a cigarette. 'Come on, Mamphela. Ministers don't approve of this sort of thing.'

'Don't they?' Mamphela said bitterly. 'If you go to him, he will find a good reason.'

Father Kani, an elderly black priest who was one of Biko's most enthusiastic supporters, turned to Dilima. 'You are sure it was Captain De Wet?'

Dilima looked a little puzzled. Father Kani repeated the question in the Xhosa language. Now Dilima answered at once, nodding his head up and down. '*Ndimbonile*,' he declared. 'I am positive.'

Crossly, Woods breathed out smoke from his cigarette. 'Where is Steve? What are his ideas about the situation?'

'He went to the clinic,' Mamphela replied. 'He wanted to take the security police away while you talked to Dilima.'

'Well, that's sensible,' Woods agreed. 'But I can't print a story from a witness who can't appear in court.'

'Any mention of Dilima's name in your newspaper,' Ntsiki warned, 'and he will never survive to appear in court.'

'I'd be surprised if he survived until the end of the week,' Mamphela added.

Wendy had heard enough. 'Donald, fly to Pretoria! The

police here will just laugh at you, but you can't let this happen without doing something.'

Woods stared at her doubtfully.

'Do it! Go!' she said.

Woods did not take a suitcase or even a bag. He phoned Kruger's office and Kruger agreed to meet him at his home outside Pretoria on Saturday. It was early afternoon when the taxi stopped at the gates of Kruger's home and Woods got out. There were no guards at the gate and Woods walked slowly up to the house, looking at the surrounding hills and the beautiful large garden.

'Ah, Mr Woods, you are here.' Kruger was standing outside the front door, very relaxed, wearing an open shirt and holding a drink. Two little dogs jumped about at his feet. 'Come in, come in. I'm just having a drink. Will you join me?'

'The Minister of Police,' Woods said, amazed, 'and I walk right into your house with no one in sight.'

'Oh, perhaps not in sight – but if you weren't expected . . .' Kruger raised his eyebrows. He led Woods into his study, a large, comfortable room.

'I want to thank you for seeing me at the weekend,' Woods said.

'*Ag*, it's nothing, man. I always like to help you editors if I can.' Kruger gave Woods a glass of whisky. 'What is it you wanted to see me about?'

'It's about Steve Biko,' Woods began, sitting down.

'Biko!' Kruger exclaimed. 'I know all about Steve Biko!'

'Why is he banned?' Woods asked. 'He believes in non-violence, and he is a black leader you can talk to. You need a leader like that.'

'Look, Mr Woods, I promise you, we have reason to ban Steve Biko.'

'If you have, then why not take him to court?'

Kruger leaned forward in his chair. 'Listen. You know we have special problems in this country and we have to do things we don't like. Do you think I like banning people and keeping people in prison without trial? Man, I am a lawyer. I don't like these things.' Suddenly he stood up. 'Come, come. I want to show you something, Mr Woods.'

He led Woods out through another door into a hall. One wall of the hall was covered with photographs, a history of Kruger's family.

'We Afrikaners came here in 1652, two hundred years before there was a camera.' He pointed to the earliest photograph, taken in the 1860s or 1870s, showing a group of men working on a farm. 'Look at the concentration camps the British put our women and children in during the Boer War.' The photographs showed starving women and children – nothing but skin and bone. 'The British never defeated us, you know, but we couldn't go on fighting when our families were dying in those concentration camps.'

There were other photographs – a farm in the 1920s, a car in the 1930s, a young man in a football shirt holding a ball, obviously Kruger himself. Kruger waited as Woods glanced at the last photographs.

'Let me tell you, Mr Woods, any Afrikaner family could show you the same thing. We built this country. Do you think we are going to give all this away? That is what Mr Biko wants. This is a black country, he says. *Gott!* What is here was made by Afrikaner work and struggle and blood.

The blacks came to us for work – remember that. We didn't force them to work.'

Woods knew the Afrikaner argument. 'No, you didn't force them to work, but since you had taken over most of the land they didn't have much choice. And wouldn't you say that their work has helped your success?'

Kruger did not answer. Instead he opened the main doors and the two men looked out at the wonderful view – the hills and a large lake that filled one of the valleys in the distance. Kruger went over to some chairs on the grass, the two little dogs following him.

'Let's sit out here in the shade,' he said. 'We know we must find a way to work together and live together. We are trying to find a way. Maybe it's a little too slow for some of them, but Mr Biko is giving them false hope. We are not just going to roll over and give all this away.'

Woods looked at the beauty of the garden and the view, and remembered the black township he had visited. The difference between the two made the threat of revolution more real than ever.

'Listen,' Kruger said quietly, leaning forward. 'Trust me. I know more about Mr Biko than you do, Mr Woods. But I shall consider your recommendation, if you really think it's worth it.'

'Thank you, Minister. I do think it's worth it. But I have really come about a community centre in King William's Town which was smashed up the other night . . .'

'*Ja*, I know about that. My police are investigating it.'

'Your police are the ones who *did* it!'

For a second Kruger froze. Then he slowly put his drink down and turned to Woods. 'What makes you say that?'

'A witness saw a police captain and some of his men smash the place.'

'And will the witness make a statement?' Kruger asked coldly.

'He's afraid to,' Woods answered, 'and I felt it would be better if you dealt with it yourself.'

Suddenly Kruger returned to his friendly attitude. '*Ag*, you are right!' he declared. 'I appreciate your helpful attitude. I shall pursue this matter. I don't want this sort of thing happening.'

Woods was surprised. The warmth and sincerity of Kruger's response impressed him. 'Well, I . . . that's it,' he said, feeling it was all too easy after his long trip from East London. He finished his drink and stood up. 'Thank you.'

'*Ag*, thank you, for the way you have dealt with this unpleasant business,' Kruger responded.

As they walked towards the house, Kruger's son, aged about fifteen, came towards them. 'Will you be able to play tennis?' he asked his father.

'*Ja*, of course,' Kruger replied. 'Johan, this is the editor of the *Daily Dispatch*, Mr Donald Woods.'

'I'm pleased to meet you,' the boy said politely.

'Did you come by car, Donald?' Kruger asked.

Woods was surprised by the sudden use of his first name. 'No, sir, by taxi.'

'I'll drive you back to the city.'

'No, no,' Woods protested. 'You have your game of tennis. If you can just call a taxi for me . . .'

'It's no trouble, man. We have all afternoon for tennis. Besides, the dogs want a ride.' He took his keys out of his pocket and the dogs immediately started jumping up at his legs. Woods was amused. It was a nice picture: the relaxed father, the polite son, the spoiled dogs.

'This is very kind of you,' Woods said, as they walked around the house to where the cars were parked.

'*Ag*, Mr Woods, we are not really the terrible characters people think we are.'

And at that moment Woods believed that was probably true.

9

On Sunday afternoon Wendy was in the kitchen and Woods was reading in the living room, when someone banged on the front door. Charlie the dog growled and ran to the door.

'All right, Evalina,' Wendy called. 'I'll get it. Charlie! Get back here!'

There were two men outside the front door. 'Yes?' she said. 'Can I help you?'

'Mr Donald Woods? Is he available?'

At that moment Woods appeared, carrying his newspaper, his glasses down his nose. He was a little annoyed at being disturbed. 'I'm Donald Woods.'

'You complained to the Minister of Police?' one of the men, Fred Lemick, asked.

Woods smiled. They were police. 'It's all right, Wendy,' he said, and Wendy took Charlie by the collar and pulled him back to the kitchen. 'That's quick! I saw Mr Kruger only yesterday.'

'You had a witness,' Lemick said.

'Yes. I explained to Mr Kruger that I couldn't name him . . .'

'You reported a crime, Mr Woods, and the law states that you must give us the name of the witness.'

Woods, who had been pleased with the minister's quick action, suddenly realized that he was dealing with a local policeman who did not understand the situation. 'I said that I explained to Mr Kruger . . .'

'You must give us the name of the witness – or you'll go to prison,' Lemick repeated. 'That is the law.'

It was too much for Woods. 'I would hate to go back to Mr Kruger,' he said sharply, 'to report that you . . .'

Lemick smiled. 'Report to whoever you like,' he interrupted. 'Our orders come from the very top.'

For a moment Woods stared at him. What did he mean, 'the very top'? Then he began to understand. 'Kruger?' he murmured doubtfully.

Lemick smiled again, confident now that he was in control of the situation. He glanced at the other detective. 'I didn't say Mr Kruger – I said from the top.'

Woods realized from the man's confidence where the order had come from, and he felt that Kruger had betrayed him. He stared angrily at Lemick. 'The next time he sends you,' he declared bitterly, 'you had better bring a warrant.'

'The law is on our side,' Lemick said confidently.

'Yes, well, justice is on my side,' Woods said angrily. 'We shall see what happens in court.' He started to shut the door but then paused. 'Oh, and tell Mr Kruger that he must come to my house for a whisky one day!'

Nothing happened for several weeks and Woods assumed that Kruger had decided not to take the matter to court. He printed a long article by Tenjy and Mapetla about the damage done to the church, and another flood of gifts poured in. Gradually, the damage was repaired. Woods decided one Thursday afternoon to drive over to the community centre to see how they were progressing. As he left the office, a court official was waiting at the door and handed him an envelope from the court.

That afternoon a group of black men were playing rugby in a lonely field outside King William's Town. As they played, a white man appeared over the hill and stood, watching them play. When the game was over the two teams started to walk up the hill towards the road, muddy but laughing. Someone saw the white figure at the top of the hill.

'Steve – it's the System!' someone warned.

Quickly, the players moved until they were surrounding Biko.

'I'll go and talk to him while you get Steve away,' someone offered.

But as they moved up the hill, Biko felt sure that he recognized that figure. 'It's OK, I think,' he said quietly. The man began to walk towards them, and then Biko was sure. 'It's OK,' he repeated loudly, and pulled away from the group.

'You're a dirty player,' Woods called.

'I was taught by a priest,' Biko called back. 'What do you expect? Are you alone?'

'All alone,' Woods replied.

'How did you know I was here?'

'Your wife told me,' Woods answered. 'She didn't tell me where the police think you are.'

Biko laughed. 'They think I'm at the clinic. I came here in the bread van.' He nodded towards a van parked a little way off the field where the other men were getting bottles of beer.

'They're taking me to court over the name of the witness,' Woods said, as they walked over to the van.

Biko stared at him in amazement.

Woods smiled. 'I think they're trying to break off our friendship.'

Biko looked at Woods for a moment. 'I don't know. A few months in prison would finish your education, I think.'

Some of the other players laughed.

'I'm getting my former law teacher, Harold Levy, to conduct my defence. But I'm not going to name Dilima, whatever happens,' Woods said. He raised a bottle of beer to Biko. 'Kruger is obviously serious,' he added, and took a long drink.

'One day *we* shall be the System in this country,' someone growled. 'Then, watch out!'

Biko sat down near Woods. 'A rotten policeman is a rotten policeman,' he said quietly. 'He breaks heads for the same reasons. Black or white, it isn't worth the price of one child . . .' There was silence for a moment, then he looked across at Woods. 'Not to talk of six months in prison for Mr Woods!'

Biko and his family lived in a tiny house in the black township outside King William's Town. One night, about a week later, Biko was working late on an article for Woods to be printed in the *Daily Dispatch* under another name. Suddenly, Ntsiki whispered a warning. Biko stopped writing and they both listened.

'There's someone out there with a torch,' Ntsiki whispered.

At that moment, someone banged loudly on the front door.

Biko gathered up the papers he was working on and Ntsiki took away the pen. According to the banning order, he was not allowed to write anything, not even a letter.

Biko went to the front door and opened it a crack, pretending to look sleepy. Lemick, the local detective, was there with Biko's two regular 'minders'.

'Yes?' Biko growled, pretending he had just woken up.

'We have orders to search your house for dangerous documents,' Lemick said aggressively.

Biko nodded coolly. Then he smiled at the two regular security police. 'They're keeping you boys up late,' he said sympathetically.

'I think the police are trying to break off our friendship,' said Woods.

Lemick was annoyed by this familiarity. 'Just open the door!'

Biko yawned. 'Do you have a warrant?'

Lemick, even more annoyed, pulled the document from his pocket and waved it in front of Biko's face.

'Good,' said Biko, in the same sleepy manner. 'Bring it to the window over there and I'll read it.' And he shut the door and locked it.

Lemick was angry, but he decided he would look a fool if he asked the two security policemen to break down the door. Sighing heavily, he walked to the side window. In the house, Biko made a quick search and gave another paper to Ntsiki, who was now holding their younger son, Samora, in her arms. Then Biko went over to the window and opened it at the top.

'I'll need your torch,' he said, yawning again.

One of the 'minders' stepped forward and shone his torch on the warrant. Biko began to read, pretending to study each word. Behind his back, Ntsiki had put a baby's nappy on their bed, laying the papers on top of it. Gently, she lifted the sleeping Samora on to the papers and fastened the extra nappy on. Samora did not wake.

At the window, Biko reached the bottom of the first page and looked up at Lemick. 'Fine,' he said. 'Turn the page, please.'

Lemick stared angrily at Biko. 'Could you read a little faster?'

Biko continued to read each word. Behind him, Ntsiki coughed, a sign that she had finished. She picked up Samora, with his double nappy, and held him against her shoulder.

Finally, Biko nodded. 'Well, it's all in order, but you won't find any papers in my house.'

Lemick folded the document and put it back in his pocket. 'We shall see.'

Biko started to shut the window. 'As soon as my wife is properly dressed, I'll let you come in.'

Lemick was angry. He went back to the door and banged loudly on it.

Slowly, Biko opened the door. 'Sssh,' he whispered. 'Don't wake the children.'

There was only one oil lamp burning, so Lemick and the two other men used their torches to search the tiny house: a bookcase, the beds, the pots and pans, the cooker. They pulled the covers off the sleeping Nkosinathi and passed their hands under his bed. Ntsiki and Biko watched.

'I told you there were no papers,' Biko remarked.

Lemick looked around angrily. He stared at Biko and then at Ntsiki.

'It's a crime they send you people out on these useless jobs,' Biko said sympathetically.

Lemick stared at Biko again, not sure if he was joking, but his face looked serious. Lemick sighed and nodded to the two 'minders'. He followed them to the door. 'We'll be back,' he said loudly.

'Sssh,' Biko whispered, nodding towards the sleeping Samora.

Lemick paused and then closed the door quietly. Steve turned to Ntsiki. She was laughing silently. She patted Samora's nappy. 'I think we had better rescue these,' she whispered.

And they both gasped with silent laughter.

The System Fights Back

10

Woods faced six months in prison if he did not give the name of Dilima to the court. If, after the six months, he still refused to give the name, he would get another six months in prison. However, Harold Levy conducted Woods' defence with confidence and Woods was released on a legal point.

Later that evening Woods was in the living room telling the children about his trial. 'At that moment, everyone in the court was silent, thinking that I was going to prison . . .'

Gavin jumped up excitedly. 'So you *are* going to prison, Dad?'

Suddenly, Charlie growled, running to the back door.

'Donald!' Wendy shouted from upstairs. 'It's the police. They're after Evalina!'

Woods put down his drink and rushed into the hall. Wendy ran downstairs. 'Keep the children inside,' Woods ordered. He went to a cupboard in the hall, reached up, and pulled open the top drawer. He took out a gun and moved towards the back door.

'Donald! What are you doing?' Wendy screamed, holding on to his arm. Charlie was jumping up at them both.

'Go to the children!' Woods ordered, shaking her off. 'And take Charlie.'

'Donald!' she cried once more, taking Charlie by the collar; but Woods was out of the back door.

He ran around the house to Evalina's room, a separate small building near the main house. Two policemen with torches were standing at Evalina's door.

'What the hell are you doing here?' Woods shouted, pointing his gun at the policemen.

Evalina appeared at her door. 'It's all right, sir. It's all right,' she called to Woods, frightened.

'We want to see her pass,' one of the policemen said aggressively. 'It is our right.'

'At this time of night?' Woods demanded.

'It's all right, sir. I'll get it,' Evalina repeated.

'We have asked this female Bantu . . .' the policeman began.

'Woman!' Woods shouted. 'She's a woman, not a female Bantu! Do you think you're talking to an animal?' His gun was still pointed at the policemen and in Woods' face was all the anger that had been growing in him since he first turned his attention to examine what South Africa was to a black man.

The policeman stepped back, beginning to lose some of his confidence in the face of Woods' aggression. Evalina had found her pass and came to the door with it.

'We are allowed to question Bantu at any time,' the policeman said. 'It's our job. There may be an illegal male inside . . .'

'You're on my property,' Woods shouted.

The second policeman, a younger, larger man, smacked his stick against his leg. 'You think you're a big editor, who can do anything you please . . .'

'I think I'm a man who has found two strangers on my property,' Woods said, waving his gun at them. 'Go on! Get out of here!'

The two policemen finally began to walk down the path towards the gate. Wendy ran out of the back door and across the garden to Woods. She put her arms around him. 'You're crazy, Donald Woods! You're a crazy man!'

'I'm also shaking like a leaf,' Woods said, putting his arm around her waist. 'And if you let go, I think I'll fall flat on my face!'

Wendy laughed, and kissed him.

The next day the police took their revenge. Ken saw it all, even got pictures of it. It was the middle of the morning and Ken went out of the office to buy ice-cream with Doreen, the prettiest typist in the office. They walked slowly along the street back to the *Dispatch* building.

Ken turned and took a spoonful of Doreen's ice-cream.

'Stop it!' she laughed. 'You've got your own ice-cream.'

'If you let me have a little bit of yours, I'll let you have some of my chocolate,' Ken offered, smiling.

He stopped. Over Doreen's shoulder he saw a black police car suddenly stop just in front of Mapetla, who was also walking back to the office. Three men jumped out and took hold of Mapetla. Ken dropped his ice-cream, took his camera from where it hung on his belt, and ran forward taking pictures. The men pushed Mapetla into the car, banged the door shut, and the car quickly drove away. One of the policemen pointed a finger angrily at Ken, but he continued taking pictures until the car turned a corner.

Later that night, after the children had gone to bed, Woods told Wendy what had happened.

'What do you think the police will do to him?' Wendy asked.

'Oh, I suppose they'll beat him, to frighten him and try to get him to leave the newspaper,' Woods replied. 'But I'm afraid they will make an example of him so that no other black person will dare to come near me.'

Wendy stood up and they both began to go upstairs to bed.

'I've decided not to print the pictures,' Woods continued. 'If I do, the police will probably be harder on Mapetla.'

Suddenly someone knocked loudly on the front door. They both stopped and looked at each other. Was it the police again? Charlie appeared and rushed to the door. Slowly, Woods went down the stairs again and went to the door.

'Steve!' he whispered as he opened the door. Biko quickly went past him into the hall. Woods glanced outside, saw only one car, and shut the door. 'What the hell are you doing here?'

'I want to know about Mapetla,' Biko replied, his face serious.

Woods nodded and nervously led him into the living room. 'God!' Woods sighed. 'Steve, I don't know – travelling into a white area at night.' He shook his head.

'This is *my* country,' Biko replied quietly. 'I go where I like.'

Woods admired Biko's attitude, but at the same time was shocked by the risk Biko was taking. At that moment Wendy came into the living room. She stood at the door, unable to speak for a moment.

Biko smiled at her amazement. 'Hello, Wendy,' he said calmly.

'You're crazy . . .'

Woods poured Biko a drink and repeated the story of Mapetla's arrest. Biko listened silently. 'I want to write something about the arrest,' he said finally. 'I'll give it to you on my way to Cape Town in a few days.'

'Cape Town?' Wendy protested.

'Steve, you're out of your mind,' Woods added.

Biko looked at the two of them and leaned back, suddenly tired, in his chair. He took a long drink. 'It's an important meeting of black students,' he explained. 'I want them to hear what I have to say before they decide anything.' There was no doubt about the importance of the meeting to him, but for once his fire and energy were gone, and he sounded exhausted.

For two days nothing happened. Woods did not print news of Mapetla's arrest, and the police refused to give him any information about Mapetla. Woods hoped that the police would release him in a few days.

But he was badly mistaken. At twelve o'clock, when the streets around the *Dispatch* were most busy, a police car and a police van with bars at the windows parked outside the office. Three policemen got out of the car and marched into the building. They went up the stairs to the newsroom and went directly to Tenjy's desk. She was typing an article but looked up and stared at them. She knew at once what was going to happen.

'I have a warrant for Tenjy Mtintso,' one policeman said. 'Are you Tenjy Mtintso?'

Tenjy nodded and bit her lip. She glanced around the room. Everyone was staring, but there was nothing anyone could do.

'Please come with us,' the policeman said.

Ken left the newsroom and rushed downstairs to look for Woods. They both ran to the front door but it was too late. The police were already closing the doors of the van on Tenjy. Ken began taking pictures as Woods pushed through the crowd and took the arm of one of the policemen.

'I would like to know what the charges are in that warrant,'

Woods said, looking at Tenjy through the bars of the little window at the back of the van.

The policeman shook off Woods' hand and looked at him with cold hatred. 'There are no charges,' he said, getting into the police car. 'We don't need charges.' And the car drove off.

The next day Woods printed the photographs of Mapetla's arrest, as well as those of Tenjy's arrest, on the front page of the *Daily Dispatch*. But for another week there was no further news.

Then late one evening Ken went to say goodnight to Woods and found him staring out of the window.

'What's wrong?' he asked.

Woods turned slowly to his desk and Ken knew that something serious had happened. Woods looked up at Ken. 'Mapetla is dead,' he announced. 'They say he hanged himself.'

Ken stared at him, unable to speak. 'Mapetla wouldn't . . .' he began, and then stopped. That was something they both knew; there was no need to say it. They sat silently in the growing darkness, filled with the bitter knowledge that they could not print the truth.

Biko, despite his sorrow, was able to demand an inquest and Wilfred Cooper agreed to represent Mapetla's family and Biko. The main witness at the inquest was Tenjy. When she appeared in the witness box, she looked tired and ill in her prison uniform.

Cooper began to question her. First her name, then her occupation.

'I was a reporter on the *Daily Dispatch*. Now I am a prisoner.'

'Charges?' Cooper asked.

'None,' Tenjy replied.

'This inquest has been called to determine the reason for the death of Mapetla Mohapi, who was found hanged in prison.'

Tenjy turned and looked bitterly at the security officer, Captain Schoeman, who was sitting in court behind the lawyer representing the State.

'Can you offer an explanation for the bruises found on the side of the dead man's neck, rather than under the neck, as would be the case if he had hanged himself?'

'Yes,' Tenjy answered at once. 'The security police question prisoners by . . .'

Cooper interrupted her gently. 'Have you heard about this from someone else?'

'No,' Tenjy answered forcefully. 'I was questioned in this way myself by Captain Schoeman and his colleagues.' She turned and fixed her eyes on Schoeman. 'First, they pulled me around the room by my hair, then beat me to the floor and kicked me. I still refused to swear to something I had not done. They tied me to a chair and put a towel around my neck. They pulled this towel tighter and tighter until I became unconscious. This happened several times and produced these bruises.' She pulled down her collar to show large bruises on the side of her neck.

Wendy was crying as she listened to this. She reached over and took Woods' hand. 'How can we get her out of there?' she whispered.

Woods did not reply. He knew no easy way.

The lawyer representing the State stood up. 'I really do find this story of a towel around the neck rather like the articles

Miss Mtintso wrote for the *Dispatch*: full of emotion but rather short on facts . . .'

Cooper interrupted. 'Perhaps Miss Mtintso could show us?' He took a towel from his bag and crossed the court to the witness box.

Tenjy looked surprised, but she took the towel and without hesitation she threw it over her face from behind and pulled it tight about her throat. As she pulled it tighter, she began to cough. Then she stopped and took off the towel. She swallowed several times, staring at Schoeman coldly and accusingly. Tears began to roll down her face.

The judge left the court for only fifteen minutes. 'The inquest finds that blame for Mapetla Mohapi's death can be fixed on no one. The inquest is closed.'

Woods stared at Wendy in complete amazement. He turned and found Mamphela looking at him, smiling bitterly. Her smile seemed to say, 'You see? What did I tell you?'

Later that night Biko phoned Woods. Woods was sitting in his office on his own, finishing his editorial on the inquest. It was quiet and in the newsroom only the light at the sports desk was still on.

'Some news,' Biko said. 'The day before Mapetla died, the police showed another prisoner a small figure of Mapetla hanging from a string.'

Woods sank back in his chair, overcome by this example of police cruelty. 'Oh, God . . .' he sighed. 'Steve, I just don't know what to say.'

'Just say,' Biko replied quietly, 'that some day justice will be done. And let us hope that it won't be visited on the innocent.' He paused and then put the phone down.

Biko had phoned from Mamphela's room, where she was

typing his article on the inquest. She had stopped typing while he made the call, aware of the deep emotion in his voice. 'You shouldn't make that trip to Cape Town,' she said. 'It's too dangerous.'

Biko looked across the table at her. 'It's a dangerous country.'

11

The road-block was put up at 10 p.m. The police changed the place and time of road-blocks because news of them travelled fast. They were never kept in place for long, either. So if you came across a road-block, it was bad luck.

On this night the road-block outside Port Elizabeth had just been put up. Only two cars had been stopped before Peter Jones – one of Biko's closest friends – drove round the bend and saw the police lights of the road-block flashing ahead. There were two police cars and a Land Rover. There was no chance of turning and certainly no chance of running through it.

Peter put his foot on the brake. 'They'll probably only ask for my papers,' he said nervously.

Biko was sitting next to him in the front seat. They were on their way back from Cape Town, driving along the main coastal road with the ocean on one side and the mountains on the other. They had driven more than half-way home to King William's Town, and had only another two hundred kilometres to go. 'Have you got anything in the back?' Biko asked.

'No. All the posters were given out in Cape Town. I've only got a spare tyre back there.'

The car ahead of them was sent on by the police and a policeman waved Peter forward with his torch. Peter slowly moved the car forward and stopped. The policeman shone the light from his torch on to Peter's face.

'Keys and papers!' he commanded.

Peter passed over his identity papers and the keys of the car. The policeman threw the keys to his colleague and then shone his torch on to the papers.

The second policeman went to the boot of the car and tried to open it. He had trouble with the lock. Biko glanced sideways at Peter. Peter shook his head, but neither of them dared to say a word.

The policeman at the window handed the papers back to Peter, satisfied, and shone his torch around the back seat. He stepped back, ready to let them go.

'I can't get it open,' called the policeman at the boot.

Instantly, the policeman at the window suspected something. 'What's in there?' he demanded aggressively.

'Nothing,' Peter answered, with desperate honesty.

Another policeman approached Biko's side of the car. 'What's the matter?' he demanded.

'I think they've got something in here,' the policeman at the boot answered.

'Can I try?' Peter asked, opening his door. The policeman at his window nodded.

But the policeman on Biko's side of the car stopped at the window. He knocked on it. 'Out!' he ordered.

Biko hesitated for a moment, but he had no choice. Slowly, he pushed open the door and got out. He stood up, much taller than the policeman, and fixed his eyes on the darkness straight ahead.

'Papers!'

Again Biko hesitated. Then he reached into his coat and handed the man his pass. The policeman shone his torch on to Biko's face and then down at the pass. Suddenly he stiffened. The light went back to Biko's face and once again to the pass.

'What's your name?' he demanded.

'It's there in the book,' Biko replied.

'Say it! Say it!' the man shouted fiercely.

The other policemen turned to look. What was happening?

There was a silent pause. Then Biko answered. 'Bantu Stephen Biko,' he said evenly. And the other policemen stared in amazement.

Six days later – again in the dead of night – a police car drove through the forest trees to the Walmer police station in Port Elizabeth. The yard was lit with bright lights, and when the car paused at the gates the guard dogs growled. The car entered the yard and a doctor got out.

The doctor was led by the chief police officer down a long corridor and through several locked doors. Finally, the last door was opened and the doctor saw a naked figure lying on the bare floor. The doctor moved forward into the room. He saw that the man's hands were tied behind his back, and one leg tied to the bars of the wall. He was breathing heavily.

The doctor went in and knelt down by the body. The body was covered with bruises, the forehead and eyes seriously injured. There were cuts on his chest and lips. The doctor examined the prisoner's eyes: he was deeply unconscious. The doctor lifted one arm; it fell back lifelessly. It was obvious that a doctor should have seen the prisoner much sooner.

The doctor turned to his bag and took out a small hammer.

He ran it lightly along the left foot. No reaction. He hit the foot once, twice. The toe moved upwards. The doctor rested the hammer on the floor for a moment, breathing heavily himself. He knew what he must recommend, but he also knew that the prisoner Biko was very important to the police.

The doctor stood up. 'I . . . I think he should go to a hospital,' he said, wishing this had been decided earlier.

The police officer looked at him coldly. 'Could he be pretending?'

My God, the doctor thought. How could you pretend a smashed forehead, or eyes swollen by the blood behind them? Even a policeman could answer that question, surely? 'The . . . the reflex indicates possible brain damage,' he began cautiously.

'*Could* he be pretending?' the police officer repeated fiercely.

'You . . . you can't pretend a reflex, sir,' the doctor replied. He looked down at the report on Biko. 'The tests performed by Dr Hersch also show . . . also have signs of possible brain damage.'

'But why is he unconscious?' the police officer demanded. He had seen other injured men who had managed to survive.

The doctor could not answer that. 'Has he eaten?'

'No, not today.'

Finally, the doctor faced the officer. 'He must go to hospital,' he said, with fear but with as much determination as he could manage.

The officer glanced down at the bruised body on the floor and then up at the white, fearful face of the doctor. 'We'll take him to the police hospital in Pretoria,' he said at last.

The doctor gasped. 'But ... but that's a thousand

kilometres away!' he protested. 'There's a hospital in Port Elizabeth, only four kilometres away!'

'He could escape from hospital here,' the officer said brutally. 'I want him in a police hospital.'

The doctor looked down at the unconscious prisoner. Escape? He would be lucky if he could walk and talk within weeks. It was obvious to the doctor that the police officer wanted police doctors to deal with the prisoner Biko. The doctor knew that he should insist on the prisoner being taken to the nearest hospital, without delay. He was determined to demand this. He looked up into the cold, angry eyes of the police officer . . . and said nothing.

Half an hour later, the doctor watched as four policemen carried Biko out into the yard. Another policeman threw a blanket on to the floor of the waiting Land Rover and Biko, still naked, was put on it.

A police captain gave the four policemen their final orders. 'I want you to take the Seymour road. Keep off the main roads. And when you stop for a rest, one man should stay with the prisoner at all times.'

The doctor expected them to cover Biko, but no. Two policemen got into the back of the Land Rover, and the other two sat in the front. Again, the doctor wanted to say something, but the police chief had his eyes fixed on the Land Rover.

The doctor watched as the doors were banged shut and the Land Rover drove off into the night, Biko's head bumping on the floor. He had one thousand kilometres of rough, country roads yet to survive.

It was 11th September 1977.

12

Someone phoned Woods in the night and told him Biko was dead. Perhaps it was one of the black prison officers, or a black worker at the police hospital. At first, Woods did not believe it. Then he received another call, from his night editor: the government had just ordered that any article on the police must be approved by the central police office in Pretoria. Woods got dressed and went to the office. On the way he tried to convince himself that it was not true. The government needed black leaders to talk to. Biko was a big name and he was known as a leader who believed in non-violence. Besides, he had been in prison before and had come out unhurt.

By the time he got to the office there was a message from John Qumza. It was true.

BIKO DIES IN CUSTODY! This was on the front page of the *Daily Dispatch* the next morning. The news was taken up by every newspaper in the country. Woods spent hours on the phone talking to friends outside South Africa so that the story was printed in almost every country in the world.

In the black townships throughout South Africa, black crowds attacked police stations. Huge fires were lit in the townships every evening until the funeral. In Crossroads, thousands marched in a procession that went on for a whole day and into the night, with drums and wild singing. Ntsiki stayed in their little house, holding Nkosinathi and Samora, and crying for Steve . . . and for herself and the boys. And they, not understanding what was wrong, cried with her.

The Minister of Police, Mr Kruger, denied police responsibility for Biko's death. Yes, Mr Biko had been arrested, outside his banning area. Once in custody, Mr Biko had refused to eat. This was why he was taken to hospital, and this was why he died: he starved himself to death.

Kruger's smiling face on television drove Woods into action. The next day Woods and Ken drove the sixty kilometres north to King William's Town, and parked in a small road just outside the town. A few minutes later a bus stopped opposite and Ntsiki got off. Woods had phoned to ask her to meet him and she had come.

It was the first time they had met since Biko's death. Ntsiki stood at the side of the road, waiting until the bus moved off again. Then she started to cross the road. Woods went to greet her. When they reached each other, they paused and looked at each other, their minds full of memories, of sympathy, and of sorrow. So much had happened since their first meeting, less than two years ago.

Then Woods moved forward and put his arms round Ntsiki. 'He was a great man, Ntsiki,' he whispered. 'A man the world will always remember.'

As they drove to the mortuary, Woods explained what he wanted to do. He had learned from Biko himself, when Mapetla died, that the family could demand an inquest. Kruger was claiming that Biko had died because he refused to eat in prison. All Biko's friends knew that was not true. The question was, how did he die? To find out, they needed Ntsiki's help. Ntsiki nodded her head, but she did not speak.

They got out of the car near the little building. 'How did you get permission?' Ntsiki asked quietly.

'I didn't,' Woods replied. 'I knew they would move him if they thought we were coming. I have checked the law. I don't think they will dare to stop us.'

A short, elderly Pakistani opened the door and led them to the main office. 'Mrs Biko wants to see her husband's body,' Woods began.

The official looked up from his desk. 'I'm afraid that's not possible. There has been no inquest – this is a special case . . .'

'It's not special at all,' Woods interrupted, 'The law is quite simple and clear. Mrs Biko has the right to see her husband's body.' The official stood up. 'Mr Biko's death', Woods continued coldly, 'has caused enough trouble already. If you want this matter on the front page of the newspapers as well . . .'

The official moved towards the door, frightened by Woods' anger. He led them to the room where the bodies were kept. Three pairs of feet were sticking out of the drawers. The official went forward and looked at the paper tied to the toe of one pair of feet. It read 'Biko'. He nodded towards the Pakistani assistant, who pulled out that particular drawer. The body was covered with a white sheet. The official left the room; Woods knew he would go straight to the phone.

Woods stepped forward and pulled down the top of the sheet. The sight of Biko's face shocked him. Biko's lips were swollen, there was a huge lump on his forehead, and bruises around his eyes. Ntsiki touched the sheet gently as she moved towards the face. When she reached Biko's face she suddenly burst out crying, putting her arm around him, her head down next to his.

'Oh, Steve . . . Steve,' she cried. 'What have they done to you?'

For several minutes, neither Woods nor Ken could move, their emotion was so great. But finally Woods put his arm around Ntsiki. 'We must hurry, Ntsiki, before he calls the police.'

Slowly, Ntsiki stood up and moved towards the door. The Pakistani assistant came forward to lead her out of the room. At the door he turned. 'Don't let them frighten you, Mr Woods,' he said, his own face full of fear.

Woods closed the door behind them and Ken took a small camera from his pocket. Quickly, he moved about the body, taking photographs from all sides. Woods pulled the sheet down, and Ken took photographs of the bruised body. Biko had not been playing rugby recently and had actually put on weight.

'Refused to eat,' Woods said bitterly. For a moment he stood above the familiar face of the man who had hated no one, who had now left this bruised body. He cried as he had never done before as an adult.

When they returned to the car, Ntsiki was sitting in the front seat, staring ahead. None of them spoke. Ken got into the back seat and Woods started the car.

'You and Wendy will come to the funeral, won't you?' Ntsiki asked quietly.

Woods hesitated. Considering what had happened to Biko, he wondered how people would react to a white man at his funeral. 'Well — would his other friends — would we be welcome?'

Ntsiki still stared straight ahead. 'Yes, Donald,' she answered. 'You and Wendy are our brother and sister.'

She still had not looked at him. 'We will be there,' he promised, and drove away from the mortuary.

The funeral was held two days later. Woods had never been

to the funeral of a black person before. He and Wendy went very early to the stadium where the ceremony was to be held, but even so there were thousands of people there before them, many of them carrying posters of Biko's face.

There were road-blocks on all the main roads, but still more and more people arrived. The mood of the crowd was angry but also sorrowful. Woods and Wendy took a place in the middle of the field. They saw no one they recognized from the clinic or the community centre, but no one showed any anger or hatred towards them. The crowd simply ignored them, as though they were not there at all.

About an hour after they arrived, a group of people came on to a big platform at one side of the field. Woods recognized officials representing the British, American, and Swedish Governments. Helen Suzman appeared and there

The mood of the crowd at Biko's funeral was angry but also sorrowful.

was a deep murmur of welcome from the crowd. Some church officials, black and white, followed. Woods recognized only Bishop Tutu. Then John Qumza came in with Father Kani and Mamphela. Finally, Ntsiki and the two boys came on to the platform and the murmur of the crowd grew until it was like the wounded cry of a great animal that was dying.

The stadium was completely full now, and Woods could see a number of white faces here and there. He turned to Wendy. 'When I despair, remind me of this. There are whites in South Africa who have been thinking a long time before we started to think.'

Suddenly they heard a song in the distance, and the procession arrived, moving slowly through the crowd and across the field towards the platform. A group of young men in uniform came first, marching and singing. The crowd began to sing with them. A group of priests followed. Then came the coffin, made of beautiful dark wood with gold letters: ONE AZANIA . . . ONE NATION. Woods knew that Azania was the name Biko's followers used for South Africa. As the coffin was carried slowly through the crowd, hands reached out to touch it.

When the procession reached the platform, the coffin was lifted on to the platform, flowers surrounding it. The song ended and there was silence.

A young man, dressed in gold and brown, stepped up to the microphone on the platform. 'We are here to express our deep sorrow for the death of one of the great men of Africa! I loved Steve Biko, but I *hate* the System that killed him!'

The crowd shouted in agreement, raising their hands. Finally, the speaker held up his arms and gradually the crowd became quiet.

'Even today,' he continued, 'the day of Steve Biko's funeral, the System in their white pride have turned away thousands who wanted to come here, simply to show their respect for Steve Biko! The buses from Soweto, from Durban, from Cape Town have all been turned away! And road-blocks have been put up to prevent others from every part of the country from entering this area!'

The crowd exploded with anger, their shouts like thunder. The posters were held high and waved backwards and forwards. Anxiously, Woods put his arm around Wendy. 'I had hoped this wouldn't happen,' he whispered.

At last the speaker's hands went up again, and the shouting stopped. When all was quiet, he said, '*But – we – are – here*!'

Again, the crowd exploded, but this time there was pride and determination mixed with their anger. The speaker walked up and down the platform, allowing the crowd to express their emotions. Then he stepped back to the microphone.

'I hate the System,' he said quietly, 'but I welcome *all* South Africans who join with us today in our sorrow for the man who gave us hope – hope in the country South Africa *could* be, the kind of country South Africa *will* be, when all men are judged as human beings, as equal members of God's family!'

This time the crowd began to clap, softly, warmly, with many shouts of '*Amen*!' Woods glanced around at the other white people he could see: students, here and there an elderly couple.

'And in hope for that day,' the speaker ended, 'when isolation and anger have changed to friendship, let us sing together the Song of Africa, that Steve Biko loved as we do.'

As he began the song, thousands of voices joined in, holding up their posters of Biko.

Nkosi Sikelel' iAfrika
Maluphankanyisw'upondo lwayo . . .

There were three white students near Woods. When they saw Woods singing, they pushed their way through the crowd to his side.

'Do you understand the words?' the girl asked.

Woods nodded, and began to sing in English as he worked the words out in his head.

God bless Africa,
Raise up her name,
Hear our prayers
And bless us . . .

Bless the leaders,
Bless also the young
That they may carry the
    land with patience,
In their youth, bless them.

Bless our efforts
To work together and lift
    ourselves
Through learning and
    understanding,
God bless us.

Woza Moya! Yihla Moya!
Come, Spirit! Descend, Spirit!
Woza Moya Oyingcwele!
Come, Holy Spirit!

Woods, Wendy and the students stood in the crowd as the beautiful song, full of emotion, ended and died on the wind ... On the platform, Ntsiki held Samora, the tears running down her face, and Mamphela, standing next to her, cried for the first time since Biko's death, as they watched the thousands of posters of Biko's face waving below them.

13

Woods did not print the photographs of Biko's body. He felt that the government would shut the newspaper if he did so, and he had an idea about how he should use them. Two days after Biko's funeral Woods flew north to Pretoria for a national meeting of editors. Wendy was alone in the house with the children, watching the news on television in her bedroom, when the phone rang.

'All right, we're coming to get you!' a voice said, and swore violently. 'We know you're alone, and we're coming to get you!'

Wendy tried to speak, but the caller banged the phone down. At that moment, someone knocked on the bedroom door and Wendy jumped in terror. It was Jane.

'I can't sleep,' she said. 'Was that Daddy?'

Wendy sighed in relief. 'No, not Daddy.'

'More threats?'

Wendy nodded. Suddenly they heard the sound of a car outside. Quickly Wendy turned off the light and went to the window, Jane following her. They saw a car parked across the road, its lights turned off. Two men ran from the car to the garden wall.

Jane moved back from the window. 'Who can we call?' she whispered.

Wendy ran for the door. 'You just stay here!'

But Jane followed her as she started to go downstairs. Suddenly, there was the sound of a gun being fired. Once! Twice! Jane screamed. Wendy was frozen with terror. The gun was fired again and again, and there was the sound of glass breaking. Then they heard a shout from outside. And finally the sound of the car being started and driven off. Wendy, shaking, put her arms around Jane.

The next morning they discovered holes from two bullets near Woods' study. One bullet had broken Wendy's bedroom window. Another had hit the wall by the front door, and the last was near the living room.

When Woods left Pretoria, he phoned Cape Town to ask Bruce McCullough to come to East London as quickly as he could. Bruce was an Australian, and one of Woods' oldest friends: they had been students together in London many years before. Woods also asked Father Kani to come to his house that evening.

They arrived about nine o'clock and sat down in the garden with a big bowl of spaghetti and plenty of bottles of cold beer.

'I want to go to America to talk about Biko and the way he died,' Woods began.

The two others stared at him. 'You're mad,' Bruce said, serving himself to spaghetti. 'If they let you out, they'll arrest you the minute you get back!'

'Look,' Woods responded, 'I've just come back from Pretoria and I can tell you there is no newspaper willing to fight the government on this matter. We must force them to have an inquest. If I start talking in America, it will really embarrass them.'

Father Kani shook his head. 'You're going to talk about Steve? I tell you, Donald, they'll stop at nothing.'

But Woods was determined. He booked his flight to Boston through New York. The day before he left he printed the pictures of Biko's body with an editorial demanding an inquest. Then he flew to Johannesburg, the largest city in

South Africa, using a false name, to catch the evening plane to
New York. Bruce met him at the airport in Johannesburg.

They walked together towards the passport desk. 'I've sent
copies of the photographs to England and America,' Bruce
told him. 'I only hope that Kruger's boys won't be waiting
here to meet you when you return.'

Woods smiled. Two soldiers stood behind the passport
desk. This was the moment. If the government was going to
stop him, it would be here. Woods gave his passport to the
official. The official glanced at it, then at Woods, and gave
it back to him. Woods picked it up and turned back to
Bruce.

'I'll phone you when I get there!' he called confidently.

He walked down the hall to the security desk. As he
approached it, a man touched his arm. 'Donald Woods?'

Woods nodded.

'We are security police,' the man said quietly.

Woods looked up and saw two other men approaching.
'Come with me,' the first man said, guiding Woods towards
an office door. A soldier came forward and stood beside the
door. Woods heard his flight to New York being announced,
and he hesitated.

'Don't worry about that,' the man said. 'You won't be on
the plane.'

'But my bags are . . .' Woods protested.

'No, they aren't,' the man said calmly. 'We've taken them
off.'

Shocked, Woods found himself in the office facing another
security officer, Lieutenant Beukes. Before Woods could say a
word, Beukes started reading from a warrant.

'You, Donald James Woods, are declared a banned person.

For a period of five years, you are forbidden to meet with more than one person at a time, except for members of your family. You are forbidden to write anything, either privately or printed. You are forbidden to enter any printing offices of any kind. You are to stay within the district of East London for a period of five years.'

Woods shook his head. 'Has Kruger gone crazy?' he murmured.

'The Minister of Police, Mr Kruger, signed your banning order himself,' Major Boshoff, the first officer, said. 'And he instructed us to take you by car to your home in East London immediately.'

Five years! Woods wondered what the *Daily Dispatch* would do. What would *he* do? Then he saw the Pretoria morning newspaper on the corner of the desk. BIKO INQUEST ANNOUNCED. He looked up at the two officers. The government was admitting that an inquest was proper, and at the same time punishing one of the people who wanted it. Well, he hated the banning, but he had got the inquest.

It was a long drive from Johannesburg to East London – more than eight hundred kilometres. Woods sat in the back seat, his bags piled around him. Beukes drove and Boshoff sat in the front seat beside him. For miles they said nothing.

Finally, Boshoff spoke. 'I knew Steve Biko, you know. Well, I met him once in a raid on Natal University. He was very intelligent – I agree with you about that.'

'Yes. He was very intelligent. Killing him was not,' Woods said bitterly. He turned and stared out at the darkness. 'And trying to cover it up with lies was stupid.'

'Well,' Boshoff replied easily, 'we don't know what happened yet, do we?'

'I saw his body,' Woods said shortly. 'He died of brain damage caused by someone hitting him on the head several times. Kruger knows that. He's had the report for weeks.'

No one spoke for a long time. Then Beukes glanced at Woods in the mirror. 'I've got two small children, Mr Woods,' he said quietly, 'and I think about the future. Tell me, what would you do?'

The words were sincere and helpless, and at that moment Woods could find sympathy for Beukes and the thousands of young Afrikaners like him. 'I have children, too,' he answered. 'But the days of a few whites controlling a black country are over. It's going to change – either in violence or in partnership. For the sake of your white children and mine, I hope that it's partnership.'

Boshoff laughed. 'With people like Biko?'

The words stabbed Woods like a knife. Partnership with Biko! What would that have been like? He remembered Biko's words, as they walked together near Zanempilo: 'We have all got to accept that South Africa belongs to all of us who live here – black and white.'

As he stared out into the darkness during that long drive home, Woods prayed that somehow Biko's ideas would be kept alive, to give hope for the future.

14

The second day he was home Woods started writing about Biko, using the typewriter in his study. A few minutes later, the police burst into the house. That is how Woods first learned that the house was bugged. Fortunately, Jane was at home and she claimed that the typing was hers. The police insisted that she sat down and typed, to prove to them that she could type. After that, Woods dared to type only when Jane was at home and reading in his study. When she was at school, Woods wrote by hand, not typewriter. Each night he hid the pages carefully.

Day and night, two security policemen sat across the road. Sometimes Ken visited and drove Woods to the beach. The two policemen followed in their car.

Woods wanted to communicate Biko's ideas, his non-violence and his views on confrontation. Soon, he found that he was writing a book about Biko. When Woods thought of Biko's death, he wondered how Biko had continued to believe that human beings are more good than bad. Biko had expected the struggle in South Africa to continue for twenty years, but he had no doubt that history was moving in the right direction. Some days Woods smiled at the thought that Biko would have called his book 'non-violent action'.

After three months, Woods finished writing. Then he invited Father Kani to the house and showed him the manuscript. On the first page Woods had put two photographs of Biko, one of him laughing and the other showing him very serious. Father Kani took the manuscript away with him, secretly, to read. Three days later he came back, and he and Woods went for a walk in the garden.

'I like what you've written,' Kani told Woods quietly, 'but you're playing with fire. If you get caught, you'll get what Steve got, and no one would ever know why.'

Woods felt deeply disappointed. 'So you think I've done it for nothing?' he sighed.

'What I think is that you should destroy what you have

written immediately, or else get yourself out of South Africa with the manuscript.'

Woods stared at him, unable to believe him. 'Leave here? Permanently?' South Africa was his home – his father's home, his grandfather's home, his children's home!

'Actually, yes,' Father Kani said. 'One or the other.'

Woods had put too much of his heart into the book to destroy it immediately. Instead, he called Bruce McCullough and asked him to come and visit him. Bruce agreed with Kani, but instead of telling Woods to destroy the manuscript, he contacted a friend in London who promised to publish it if it reached London.

A few days later, Woods and Wendy took the children to one of the many beaches on the East London coast. The security policemen followed them but stayed on the hill when the family went down to the beach. It was deserted. While the children played in the sand and the waves, Woods told Wendy that they must leave South Africa so that the book on Biko could be published in England.

Wendy stiffened, and stared at Woods angrily. 'I don't believe this!' she said fiercely. 'Because you want to publish a book, you're going to tear the children from their schools, their grandparents, their whole life?'

Woods was totally unprepared for Wendy's reaction. 'They're children, they'll . . .'

'You don't even bother to ask me what *I* want to do! Maybe we hate the way this country is governed, but it's still our country!'

Woods began to get angry himself. 'Wendy, do you just want to accept Steve's death? Accept what the government is doing?'

'What more do you want?' Wendy shouted. 'You've got the

inquest! You're banned! Are you going to change the government all on your own?'

'I'm going to do what I can!' Woods shouted back at her. 'I'm a writer! Do you think I can just sit for five years and not write a word?'

'And what would we do? Where would we go? Donald, we've got five children!'

'We'll survive. I'm not . . .'

'I know you! You'll tear our lives apart just to see "Donald Woods" on the cover of a book!'

Woods jumped to his feet. He had never hit Wendy, never even thought of hitting her, but at that moment he had to get away while he could still control his anger. He turned and walked away down the beach, the security policemen watching him. He walked for half an hour, trying to cool down. It was true that he very much wanted the book to be published. But it was only part of the truth. In his mind Steve Biko was the greatest man he had ever met, and that his life should end unnoticed seemed to Woods a crime, almost as great a crime as his murder.

Finally, Woods walked back to Wendy who was still sitting on the sand. He sat down near her, but she did not move or even look at him.

'Wendy, can we talk this over?' he asked quietly.

She looked at him and he saw that she had been crying. 'I'm sorry I was so cruel,' she said at last.

Woods shook his head. 'No, it's true that I want a book published. But . . . but if Steve died for nothing, if they just bury his name, if things are just going to get worse . . .'

Tears came back into Wendy's eyes, but her voice was quiet. 'Who do you think you are? God?'

Woods sighed and stared out over the shining blue sea. 'No, but there's no writer who knows Steve's story or this government like I do.'

'There are seven of us, Donald! You're forty-three years old! What is one book going to do?' She glanced over her shoulder at the security policemen watching them. 'Do you think they'll let us out? We could all get killed, trying to escape – or end up in prison for years. And your book still wouldn't be published.'

'I'm not God,' Woods said, 'but we know what this country is like now. We can't just accept it and we can't wait for God to change it. We have to do what we can – and the book is what I can do.'

What he said was sincere, touching the truth deep within him, and it reached Wendy. She turned to him, her face full of love mixed with disagreement. Finally, she leaned across the sand towards him. Woods put his arms around her as she cried again.

From the top of the hill, the security policemen still watched them.

Nothing was said about leaving South Africa for more than ten days. Wendy knew that Woods still wanted to leave, and he knew that she still did not want to leave. Then one afternoon, when Wendy was playing the piano and Woods was rewriting part of the book which might never be published, the postman knocked at the front door.

Mary ran to the door, Charlie the dog following her. 'Mummy! Daddy!' Mary called excitedly. 'It's for me and Duncan! A parcel!'

Duncan rushed out of the living room. 'It's true, Mum! Can we open it?'

Wendy continued playing the piano. 'Of course, if it's for you.'

Duncan tore open the parcel and held up a T-shirt. There was a picture of Biko printed on the front. It was a very small shirt, and he handed it over to Mary.

'I'm going to try it on,' Mary said, and ran to the mirror in the hall.

Woods came out of his study as Duncan held up the second T-shirt. 'Look, Wendy,' Woods called. 'I wonder who sent them? Is there a return address on the box?'

A desperate scream shocked them all. Mary was standing with the T-shirt over her head. She was holding her arms straight out and screaming in pain. Woods and Wendy ran to her and Evalina rushed out of the kitchen. Woods pulled the T-shirt off Mary's head. The skin on her face was bright red and swollen, her eyes half-closed. Still screaming, she started to rub her eyes.

'Don't touch your eyes!' Woods shouted, holding her hands. 'Wendy, call Dr James – ask him to come immediately!'

Wendy ran to the phone and Woods picked up Mary and carried her to the kitchen. She went on screaming as Woods and Evalina splashed water on her face and shoulders.

Duncan had dropped the shirt he was holding, but stood at the door shaking his hands. 'What's the matter? What is it?'

'Go and wash your hands!' Evalina said. 'Quickly!'

Duncan rubbed his hands on his chest. 'My hands are hurting. Why did they make the shirts that way?'

'Duncan!' Woods shouted. 'Didn't you hear what Evalina said? Go and wash your hands!'

Duncan burst into tears.

Later that night, Wendy went to kiss Duncan as he lay in bed. Bandages covered both his hands.

'You'll be all right, dear,' she said. 'Dr James said it should stop burning in a day or two. That medicine will help you to sleep well, Dr James said.'

When Wendy went into Mary's room, Woods and Jane were standing near her bed. She was sleeping, bandages on her arms and shoulders, her red, raw face covered with a white powder.

Jane was crying. 'Even if they hate us, how could they do that to her?' she whispered.

Wendy put her arms tightly around Jane, looking down at Mary. Finally, she glanced up at Woods. 'I think I want to see that book published,' she said, tears filling her eyes.

Donald put his arms around both of them.

'Even if they hate us, how could they do that to Mary?'

Escape from South Africa

15

Things happened very fast after that. Bruce McCullough and Father Kani helped Woods to plan his escape: he told no one else. One day in December – early summer in South Africa – Woods went to the bottom of the garden and climbed over the wall. He checked carefully to see that there were no security police watching that part of the house. He ran across the field and on to the side street. A car was parked on the corner. Woods ran up to it, opened the door and got in.

Bruce jumped in surprise. 'I expected you the other way!'

'If I go out the front way, they know not only where I'm going, but also who I'm with,' Woods explained as Bruce drove off.

Bruce reached into his pocket and handed a passport over to Woods. 'It's an old one, but we've altered the date. It wouldn't get you out of Johannesburg, but up north it should be OK,' he said confidently.

Woods opened the passport. '*Father* David Curren!' he laughed. 'An Irish priest! How did you get it?'

'Father Kani got it,' Bruce answered. 'He says that he's sure Father Curren would agree, but he will explain it to him later.'

Woods shook his head in amazement. 'Black hair, no glasses. But I suppose it could work.'

They drove into the country. There was no car in sight when Bruce parked by the side of the road. They got out and Bruce opened the map.

'Trying to fly you all out to Botswana is impossible,' Bruce began. 'We can't get a plane without letting someone know what's going on.'

Disappointed, Woods was silent. He could never leave Wendy and the children behind.

'Don't worry, Kani and I have planned it all,' Bruce went on confidently. 'We think 31st December is the best day. Everyone will be having parties and drinking, and the police won't be so careful. You turn yourself into Father Curren and get up north of Queenstown. Kani will meet you and drive you to the Lesotho border. You will cross the river Telle into Lesotho at night and I'll be waiting to drive you to Maseru, the capital of Lesotho. You can fly from there to Botswana. There are three planes in Lesotho.'

Woods studied the map again. It was a hundred and fifty kilometres from East London to Queenstown. 'I don't understand why I have to go so far north to meet Father Kani.'

'The police think weapons are coming into the country up there, so Father Kani wants to get a local car which the police aren't likely to check when you drive to the border.'

Woods was still doubtful. 'I don't see how I'm going to get north to Queenstown.'

Bruce laughed. 'You hitch-hike, Father Curren. You hitch-hike! That way, if you do get caught, you don't take Kani and Wendy down with you.'

Woods sighed. There seemed to be so many risks. 'What about Wendy and the children?'

'Kani has planned all that,' Bruce said enthusiastically. 'And I'm getting the newspaper to fly me from Cape Town to do a story on Lesotho's three planes.'

Five days later Woods met Father Kani to arrange the final

details of the escape plan. Kani would wait for Woods at a bridge six kilometres north of Queenstown, on the Pretoria road. Wendy would pretend to go to the beach the next morning, 1st January, but really she would drive the two hundred kilometres north-east to her parents in Umtata. She would wait there until ten o'clock for Woods to phone from Lesotho. Then she would drive on to the Lesotho border before the police realized what had happened.

31st December was a warm, sunny day in East London. Woods dyed his grey hair black and dressed in a black suit with a priest's white collar. He took the manuscript from its hiding place and packed it in a small bag. Then he took off his glasses, as the final part of his disguise; Father Curren did not wear glasses.

It was five o'clock. The younger children were playing in the living room. Jane and Dillon, who knew about the escape plan, kissed Woods goodbye. Because the house was bugged, they struggled to control their tears.

'I must go out now and pick up that film the children want to watch tonight,' Wendy said loudly and went out of the kitchen through the door to the garage.

Woods paused. He fought back his tears, looking at the kitchen for the last time – the house, his life, his children. Silently, he followed Wendy into the garage. Wendy opened the back door of the Mercedes and Woods got in and stretched out on the floor. Wendy threw a blanket over him, nervously making sure he was covered. Then she shut the door and went to open the garage.

There was only one man watching from the other side of the street – a black security policeman. Obviously Bruce was right: today was a day for parties. The man stood up to watch

Wendy. She was so nervous that she could not start the car for several minutes, but at last they drove on to the road. As they drove through town, she glanced constantly in her mirror, but no one was following them.

'You'd better sit up now, Father Curren,' she said at last, as they reached the main road north to King William's Town.

Woods sat up and picked up his coat and bag. 'You're a very brave woman, Mrs Woods,' he said warmly.

'No, I'm not!' she answered, staring at the road ahead. 'I'm a very frightened woman! And don't tell me anything else!'

She stopped the car at the end of a long line of hitch-hikers. 'No goodbyes,' she said tightly. 'Just get out, Father Curren. And I wish you luck.'

Woods looked into her eyes, knowing that she was close to tears. 'Thank you for the ride, Mrs Woods,' he said, in his best Irish accent. He shut the door and Wendy started to move off.

Suddenly, Woods ran after her, banging on the window. 'Wendy! Wendy!' he shouted desperately. She stopped and opened the window. 'Don't forget to go and collect the film.'

Wendy gasped. 'I'd forgotten all about it. Thank God you reminded me!'

Woods watched her turn the car and drive back towards the town. The afternoon had become cloudy, and now it began to rain. Woods put on his coat, then turned and went to join the line of hitch-hikers.

The journey north was not easy. After his first ride, Woods had to wait a long time before someone stopped and took him through King William's Town up the hilly road as far as Stutterheim. Then he had to wait again. It was 3.50 a.m. before he finally stepped down at the place beyond Queenstown where he hoped to meet Father Kani. It was still raining and Woods walked forwards cautiously in the darkness towards the bridge. As he approached, he saw the flash of a torch.

'I expected you three hours ago!' Kani exclaimed anxiously. 'It will start to get light in an hour's time and we still have two hundred kilometres to drive.'

'I've been in such terror that I'm surprised my hair hasn't turned grey again,' Woods responded.

Kani laughed and opened the door of the car. 'This ground was dry when I parked here. Now it's going to be difficult to get out of the mud.'

As fast as he could, Father Kani drove the little car through the darkness and the rain, the road climbing higher and higher, leaving the forest trees behind. A police car followed them for about five minutes, before turning off down a side road. Woods and Kani breathed a sigh of relief. At last, Kani turned off the main road, and then down a small, dirt road which descended to the edge of the river Telle. Silently, they got out of the car and stared at the river, wide and deep, full of rushing water. There were mountains on the other side. Lesotho.

Woods dropped his bag in disgust. The river was too fast and too wide for him to walk across. The rain had spoiled the plan. Woods saw that the sky was beginning to grow light, and he turned to Father Kani.

'You must go,' he said urgently. 'It's getting light and you'll get ten years in prison if you're seen with me.' Father Kani hesitated. 'Go, before we're seen together!' Woods picked up his bag, and as he did so, the handle broke. 'Oh, no!' he exclaimed.

'In fact, it's turned into a complete disaster, hasn't it?' Kani said hopelessly.

Woods began to move along the river. 'We've done all right. I'll find somewhere to cross. Just get out of here!'

Father Kani glanced up at the sky. Light was appearing behind the mountains. He should get the car away from the river. 'If you get desperate,' he shouted, 'go to one of us! Use Steve's name!'

Woods held the bag tightly under one arm. He waved. 'See you in London!' he called.

After Father Kani had gone, Woods tried to cross the river. He took off his shoes and tied them around his neck. He plunged into the water. In a few steps the water was up to his knees. Cautiously, he moved forward and the water reached his waist. He lifted the bag and held it on his head. He went forward again, but when the water was around his chest he stopped. He was only a third of the way across and the water was moving so fast that he knew it would be difficult to swim, even without the bag. He turned around and slowly went back to the edge of the river. It was 6.05 a.m.

16

Twenty minutes after Woods had tried to cross the river, two black hands held his manuscript. The elderly face of Tami Vundla examined the two photographs of Steve Biko. Tami slowly read the first page of the manuscript and then he turned to the very last page and read that.

Woods had found the village as he walked north along the beautiful Telle valley. He had knocked on Tami's door by chance and had explained that he was trying to cross the river. An expression of doubt had passed over Tami's face, so Woods had brought out the manuscript, hoping that it would help Tami to believe his story. Now, he sat with an old blanket round his shoulders while his clothes dried in front of the fire.

At last Tami stopped reading. 'If there is no more rain, you will find a place to cross the river tonight.'

'I can't wait,' Woods said anxiously, looking again at his watch. 'I don't have time.' Tami did not move. Suddenly Woods had a desperate idea. 'How far is the Telle Bridge?' he asked.

'Fourteen ... fifteen kilometres,' Tami answered. 'You cannot cross there.'

'I have a passport,' Woods said. 'Maybe I can. I'm so close, I can't fail now.'

Tami stood up and put the manuscript back in the bag. Then he took off his own belt and tied it around the bag. Woods felt sure that this action indicated that Tami was going to help him.

'Is there someone we can trust who has a car?' Woods asked.

Tami's face remained serious. 'I trust me,' he replied. 'And *I* have a car!' He began to laugh. 'Editor Donald Woods, escaping in my car! If Prime Minister Vorster knew . . .!'

The car was parked behind the little house. It was old, very old, but the engine finally started and they moved off, dust and leaves flying behind them. Tami was not an expert driver and he steered the car from side to side of the road. He smacked his hand on Woods' bag and laughed again. 'You will get there!' he shouted. 'You will get there! And then Vorster will know! *Mayibuye iAfrika*! Rise again, Africa!'

After another twenty minutes, the road began to curve and Tami gradually stopped the car and turned off the engine. Woods heard the sound of rushing water.

'Where is the bridge?' Woods enquired.

Tami pointed through the trees. He was quiet now, clearly frightened by the closeness of authority and danger. Woods got out of the car and walked a little way through the trees. He saw that the road descended to the river and the Telle Bridge only a few hundred metres away. He went back to the car.

'Have you seen it?' Tami asked.

Woods nodded. 'Some day, when things have changed, I will come back and we shall drink beer together, Tami.'

'Yes, Mr Woods,' Tami said, seriously. 'I shall wait for you.'

Woods picked up his bag and waved goodbye. As he walked down the hill he heard the noisy old engine start and move away. Woods came out of the trees on to the road in front of the bridge. A large iron gate blocked the road at the start of the bridge. Woods went up to it. It was locked. He shook it, but there was no sign of anyone.

Suddenly he heard the sound of a car coming down the hill behind him. It seemed to be approaching very fast. Was it someone with a message about him? Had they caught Father Kani? A Land Rover came into sight. Woods looked right and left but there was no escape. He stood there, trapped, as the Land Rover drove towards him. It stopped right in front of Woods.

A black man, wearing a brown uniform, sat in the driver's seat. 'It's locked?' he shouted.

Woods hesitated. 'Yes.'

The man looked at his watch. 'It should be open. It's seven o'clock.' He opened the door of the Land Rover, and Woods read the words painted on the door: LESOTHO POSTAL SERVICE. Woods sighed with relief.

'What are you doing on foot, Father?' the man asked.

'Well . . .' Woods began. 'A . . . a friend brought me. I . . . I must get to Maseru by ten o'clock.'

'You'll be lucky!' the man said. 'The rain has damaged the roads over there.' He looked at Woods for a minute. 'Here, Father, put your bag in here. I'll give you a ride over.'

Woods was relieved. A ride across would look more normal to the border officials than walking. 'Thank you very much. My name is . . . Curren.'

'My name is Moses,' the man said brightly.

Woods stared at him in amazement. 'Moses?'

Moses smiled. 'Yes, sir.'

Woods glanced at the river, with its fast, deep water. 'Yes, of course. It would be!'

The Telle Bridge was not a busy place. Woods and Moses were first in the queue on the South African side of the bridge. When the passport office was opened, Woods handed his passport to the official.

'We're both in a hurry,' Moses told him.

'You're always in a hurry,' the official joked. 'So tell me, why does it take four days for a letter to get from Queenstown to Maseru?'

Moses threw his passport down on to the desk. 'You know why? Because we have to spend so much time sitting outside your gate. That's what the trouble is!'

The official gave Woods his passport back and glanced at Moses' passport. Then they both moved to the door.

'Father!' the official called.

Woods froze.

'You're a brave man, Father.'

Woods stared at him, his face turning white. What did he mean?

'Driving with Moses, I mean,' the official explained. 'I wish you luck, Father. You'll need it.'

The blood began to return to Woods' face, and he left the building. Outside, a black frontier policeman was standing by the Land Rover holding Woods' bag. Moses ran to get into the driver's door, but Woods just stared at the policeman.

'Is this your bag, Father?' the policeman enquired.

'Yes,' Woods answered stiffly.

'What's in it?'

Moses was already at the wheel, waiting impatiently. For a moment Woods was speechless, then he shook his head. 'Oh, just some . . . clothes, a Bible.'

'I *thought* I felt a book of some kind,' the policeman said with a big smile, and handed over the bag to Woods.

Woods nodded and got into the Land Rover. Slowly, Moses drove across the bridge, passing the frontier and into Lesotho. Woods felt in his pocket and pulled out his glasses. At last he could put them on!

A Lesotho official stopped the Land Rover. Woods looked out, anxious again. 'A message for you, Moses,' said the official. 'There's some trouble on those roads.'

Moses parked the Land Rover and jumped out. 'I won't be long, Father.'

'Moses!' Woods called. 'Do you think I could make a phone call from here?'

Moses laughed. 'You're in Lesotho now! There's no

telephone here, unless you want to go back to the South African side.'

A terrible thought hit Woods. 'Aren't there any phones in this part of Lesotho at all?'

'The next place with phones is Maseru,' Moses said. 'If you want to phone quickly, you'd better go back to the South African side.'

'No, no. Maseru will be fine,' Woods said.

Moses nodded and went off to the Lesotho passport office for his message. Woods opened the door and looked down at the ground. The ground of Lesotho. He stepped down on it. Then he turned and looked back across the river. There it was – South Africa, the South African frontier police, the South African passport building. He turned again and looked at the wet green hills of Lesotho.

'I'm free, Steve Biko. If only you were here with me today, my friend.'

'I'm here,' he said to himself. 'I'm free, Steve Biko. If only you were here with me today, my friend.'

Suddenly, Woods started to dance, an old African dance he had learnt as a child. And as he danced, he kept repeating 'Oh God, oh God, I'm here! I've got here!'

And then, as he turned, he saw Moses and the Lesotho official watching him, their mouths open in surprise.

Meanwhile, Wendy was on the road to Umtata with the children. During the night she had packed suitcases and put them in the car. She had woken the children early and told them they were going to the beach for the day.

'And be quiet. Your father's sleeping late,' she told them, for the benefit of those who were listening.

The one security policeman was surprised to see the garage door open so early. He frowned and glanced at his watch. He looked at the children, with their beach things, as the Mercedes passed him, and did not notice the tears rolling down Jane's face.

They drove for a while, and then Duncan, realizing they were not on the road to the beach, called out, 'Mum, I think you're lost!'

And so at last Wendy told the younger children what was happening. 'So you see,' she finished, 'Daddy was really travelling all night.'

'But why are we going to Granny's?' Duncan asked.

'Because if Daddy gets across safely, he'll phone us and we'll join him and fly to England.'

Gavin leaned forward. 'What's going to happen to Charlie?' he asked anxiously.

They all looked at Wendy, waiting. 'I've left a note for

Evalina,' she said tightly. 'She'll take him to the neighbours.'

Jane glanced at her. 'What about Evalina?'

Wendy bit her lip, her eyes filling with tears. 'I don't know,' she said finally. 'Daddy has left her as much money as he could.'

They had terrible luck with the traffic. For four kilometres the roads were being repaired, with the result that no one could overtake. Then, as the road began to descend steeply, Wendy found herself behind a slow tractor. Time and again she tried to overtake, as they went down into the valley and then again as they drove up through the acacia trees on the other side; but she could never do it safely.

Jane was as nervous now as Wendy. 'Mum, we'll never get there before ten o'clock!'

'We mustn't have an accident! And we mustn't get stopped by the police!' Wendy said sharply.

But at last she was able to overtake the tractor, and the hill ahead was clear.

'Are we going to get there in time?' Gavin asked uneasily.

Wendy glanced desperately at the clock. 'I don't know. Once we get to the top, it's mainly flat – but I don't know.'

'What if we *don't* get there in time?' Duncan asked.

'Duncan! I don't know!' Wendy shouted.

At last they climbed out of the valley and Wendy began to drive faster than she had ever driven before. The three boys in the back seat leaned forward, watching the road.

'Mum . . . police,' Duncan said suddenly.

The police car was coming towards them. Wendy put her foot on the brake. Her speed went down to 88 kilometres per hour. 'Get down in the back,' she said. 'Maybe the police are looking for a Mercedes with five children in it.'

Obediently, the three boys went down on the floor. The police car passed, the two policemen glancing at Wendy. Wendy, watching them in the mirror, still drove slowly. Then she glanced at the clock: 9:45. She began to drive faster again, across the grassy hills to Umtata.

17

In Lesotho, Moses drove Woods along the main road to Maseru. To his horror, Woods learnt that there were five different roads to Maseru. How was he to know which road Bruce was on? So he was relieved when, at the first corner, there was a car parked by the side of the road.

'Is that your man?' Moses asked.

'Maybe,' Woods answered.

Moses stopped the Land Rover and Woods jumped out. The car was covered with mud, and as he approached Woods saw that the driver was sleepng. He went closer. It was Bruce!

Woods banged on the window. 'Wake up! Bruce! Wake up!

Bruce opened his eyes sleepily.

'Wake up!' Woods shouted again.

Finally, Bruce opened the door. 'At last! I thought you would never get here!'

Woods turned and waved at Moses. 'Thanks, Moses! It's the right one.'

'Good luck, Father,' Moses called as he drove off.

Woods got into the car. 'We've got to move fast. Moses says the roads are bad because of the rain.'

Bruce looked at his watch. 'Eight thirty. It took me two hours from Maseru yesterday, and I was driving fast.'

He started the car, a BMW, and got it on to the road. In the first four hundred metres Woods realized he was in the hands of an expert driver. In no time at all, the BMW passed Moses and drove on to Maseru. It was a hundred kilometres of hilly roads, with the great Lesotho mountains on their right.

When they saw the first buildings of Maseru it was 9.56. Bruce kept his eyes on the road and did not reduce his speed. As they approached the centre of the town, with its buildings of red stone, Woods saw a man wearing a suit and carrying an umbrella. He might have the information Woods needed.

'Excuse me!' Woods called, jumping out of the car as Bruce stopped. 'Can you tell me where the American or British offices are?'

The man looked calmly at Woods and then pointed his umbrella. 'The British High Commission? It's there on the right.'

Woods saw the British flag and began to run towards the building. He ran up the steps past a guard who looked at him in surprise. Inside the building a receptionist sat behind a large desk.

'I must see the High Commissioner at once,' Woods gasped. She did not move. 'My ... my name is Donald Woods,' he explained. 'I'm the editor of the South African *Daily Dispatch*.'

The receptionist looked at him doubtfully, and put her cigarette to her mouth. At last, she picked up the phone. 'There's a Father Donald Woods, an editor, to see the High Commissioner.'

'I'm not a Father,' Woods whispered.

'Yes, sir. The *Daily* . . .' she looked up at Woods.

'*Dispatch*,' he said softly.

'*Dispatch*,' she repeated, and then nodded. 'Yes, sir.' She carefully put the phone down and turned to Woods. 'The High Commissioner is in London, but the Acting High Commissioner will see you.'

She pointed to the door behind her and Woods hurried to it. As he rushed in, the Acting High Commissioner, James Moffat, came across the room to greet him.

'I didn't realize you were a priest!' Moffat exclaimed.

'I'm not, but I desperately need to use your phone.'

Moffat was surprised, but he sensed the urgency. He pointed to the phone on his desk. 'Please,' he said. 'We understood you were banned?'

'I was. Can I phone South Africa direct?'

'Yes, yes. Would you like a cup of tea?' Moffat asked kindly.

Woods smiled and shook his head. 'I've come to ask you to let me and my family enter your country,' he said as he finished dialling.

Moffat was still rather puzzled, but he bowed. 'Our pleasure,' he responded with a little smile.

'What time is it?' Woods asked, looking at his watch.

Moffat glanced at the clock on the wall behind Woods. 'Just after ten.'

Woods listened anxiously as the phone at the other end went on ringing.

In Umtata, Wendy's mother hurried in from the garden to answer the phone. 'It's all right, dear,' she called to her husband. 'I'll answer it. Yes, hello? Donald!' she exclaimed.

At that moment she heard a car approaching. She looked out of the window and saw the white Mercedes driving up to the house. 'This is strange – Wendy is just arriving. I'll call her.' She went to the open window. 'Wendy! The phone!'

Wendy got out of the car and ran towards the house, the children following her.

'Donald?' Wendy's mother said, with some concern. 'You haven't quarrelled, have you? She's got all the children with her. No, no, don't say anything. She's coming now.'

Wendy came into the room. Little Mary rushed past her, straight into her grandmother's arms. 'It's Donald,' Wendy's mother explained cheerfully.

Afraid to pick it up, Wendy stared at the phone. Was he in Lesotho, or had he failed to get across?

'Go on, Mum,' Dillon urged.

Slowly, Wendy moved to the phone.

'What's the matter?' Wendy's mother asked uneasily. 'Is something wrong?'

Wendy did not answer. She picked up the phone. 'Donald?'

Woods exploded with relief. 'Wendy! I'm here! Come as quickly as you can.'

After all her control, Wendy finally burst into tears. 'He's there!' she said to Jane and Dillon. 'He got across. Donald, shall we cross at Telle Bridge?'

'Yes. It's a sleepy little place, I can tell you. From Umtata you'll have good roads most of the way, but just hurry!'

'We're on our way,' Wendy promised. 'I love you.'

'I'm a priest,' Woods responded. 'You can't talk to me like that! Hurry!'

Wendy wiped her tears, smiling. 'Children, all go to the toilet, quickly,' she ordered. 'Mum, have you got some fruit we could take?'

Her mother turned to go to the kitchen. 'We'll drive you,' she called over her shoulder.

18

James Moffat acted quickly as soon as he understood what Woods' problem was. They would need Lesotho's permission to fly out of the country. Chief Jonathan, Prime Minister of Lesotho, was very courageous in acting independently of South Africa, but his country was dependent on South Africa. Moffat contacted one man who would be sympathetic to a liberal white South African. The man was John Monyane and he agreed to come to the British High Commission.

Monyane listened to Moffat's description of the situation and then took the manuscript on Biko. He spent about ten minutes reading a passage here, a passage there, while Woods walked nervously up and down the other side of the room, glancing out now and then at the rain that was still falling.

Finally, Monyane took off his glasses and put the manuscript down on Moffat's desk. He looked at Woods without saying anything.

Bruce looked from Woods to Monyane, and thought that neither of them was going to begin. 'They can't stay here,' he observed. 'They would never be safe from the South African police.' It was true that the South African Government often sent their police into Lesotho.

'We had hoped to fly to Botswana,' Woods added. 'The sooner the better.'

Monyane frowned and pointed at the map of southern Africa on the wall of the High Commissioner's office. 'To fly anywhere out of Lesotho,' he began, 'you have to fly five hundred kilometres over South Africa. And the South African Government demands that all planes leaving Lesotho land in South Africa before going on.'

Desperately, Woods looked at Moffat. There must be a way! 'If we flew out anyway, could they force us to land?' he asked.

Moffat shook his head helplessly. 'The law is the law.'

'They are not short of planes to force you down,' Monyane remarked.

Woods felt trapped. He had to get Wendy and the children somewhere safe when they arrived. 'My wife and children will reach Telle Bridge in a few hours. At least, can we meet them there?'

Monyane waved towards the window. 'In the rains' – he shook his head – 'impossible. But I will make sure that someone meets them and brings them safely here.'

It was raining heavily at Telle Bridge. Wendy's parents drove them the two hundred kilometres north through the hills in their van, in case the Mercedes caused problems with Customs officials. When they arrived at the bridge, Wendy and the children ran through the rain to the passport building and pushed open the door.

Wendy shook the rain from her hair and faced the passport official with a pretence of confidence. 'I'm taking the children over on a little holiday,' she explained.

The official shook his head at the crazy things people do. 'You picked good weather for a holiday,' he murmured, pushing a paper at her. 'Please write your personal details here. You can include the names of all the children, if they are under eighteen.'

Wendy smiled at him nervously and wrote quickly.

'You haven't put down your husband's name?'

'Oh . . .' Wendy hesitated. 'James.'

'OK.' The official wrote it down for her. 'And his middle initial?'

'D,' Wendy said positively.

The official glanced at her passport and handed it back to her. 'Have a good holiday. And try to stay dry.'

They went out into the rain again. Wendy's mother had found an umbrella in the van, and the boys got out the suitcases. As they began to walk across the bridge, Wendy realized how strange they must look to the frontier police. She glanced back at her parents, standing in the rain next to the van, the lights from the passport building throwing long shadows across the road.

'You haven't put down your husband's name, Mrs Woods.'

'God bless you!' her mother called, her voice full of emotion.

Wendy waved the umbrella and moved on with the children. They reached the middle of the bridge. 'Mum!' Jane suddenly called, pointing to the ground. A painted line marked the frontier, and Wendy felt a wave of relief when all of them had crossed that line.

She looked ahead to the Lesotho side of the bridge. One light shone in the darkness and under it stood a young man holding a huge umbrella and smiling brightly at Wendy. As they came closer, they could see a Lesotho Government Land Rover behind the young man, with two soldiers who were also smiling at them.

Jane passed the suitcase she was carrying to her other hand and put her arm around Wendy's waist. Wendy leaned down and kissed the top of her head as they walked on towards that huge umbrella.

The next morning, having heard the news that his wife and children were safely in Lesotho, Woods washed the dye from his hair, bought a new tie and went with Bruce to the airport. They met Mr McElrea, a Canadian, who was the boss of the three planes that flew out of Lesotho. He said that he would risk one plane, if its pilot was willing to fly out without landing in South Africa. Richie De Montauk, from New Zealand, was called into the office. Without a moment's hesitation, he agreed to make the flight.

Woods and Bruce waited at the airport while Richie and two mechanics prepared the plane. They had decided to fly south-west of Johannesburg – not the normal route – and then on into Gaberone, the capital of Botswana. Woods was walking up and down near the plane when the car arrived, bringing his family.

Jane and Mary jumped out first. 'Daddy! Daddy!' they screamed.

Then the boys rushed out of the other side of the car. 'We're here! We got across!'

Woods held out his arms and the children rushed into them. Wendy stood watching for a moment, then she, too, ran forward and kissed him.

Richie's plane was finally ready and the family began to board. Dillon gave Woods his bag, still tied with Tami's old belt. 'You should have bought a new bag when you bought your new tie, Dad,' he said.

Woods held on to the bag. 'Oh no. This goes with me – just as it is – all the way.'

'Donald!' Wendy called suddenly.

Woods turned and saw Moffat and McElrea hurrying towards them. Woods took Jane's arm. 'Help Dillon with the other bags,' he said, and went to meet Moffat and McElrea.

'The South African Government knows about the flight,' Moffat said. 'They have refused to allow the plane to fly over South Africa. If you do, they will force the plane down.'

Shocked, Woods glanced at Wendy.

'I don't think they mean it,' McElrea said. 'The newspapers of the world know about this now, thanks to Bruce, and I don't think they would dare.'

'Listen, they don't care about newspapers,' Bruce argued. 'Donald has already made them look like fools.'

Richie began to test the engines of the plane and Woods had to shout. 'Have we got a chance at all?' he asked McElrea.

'It's cloudy,' McElrea answered. 'Richie's a clever pilot. I would say you've got a chance. But the longer you wait, the more time you give them to plan something.'

Woods hesitated, and at that moment a large black car approached them. John Monyane stepped out.

'Mr Woods,' Monyane shouted above the noise of the engines. 'Chief Jonathan has arranged United Nations passports for all of you, and he has decided that I should accompany you to Botswana. It might make the South Africans hesitate. We are not sure, but it is the best we can offer.'

Woods could hardly believe the generosity of this action, but already Monyane was walking quickly towards the plane.

A few minutes later the plane was in the air. 'How long before we are over South Africa?' Woods shouted, looking down at the river below.

'Thirty seconds!' Richie shouted back. 'Maseru is right on the border. But I'm going to fly in these clouds for a while.'

They flew through the clouds for some time. Then there were voices on Richie's radio. 'They've picked up the flight,' he shouted. 'They're demanding to know who is on the plane.'

Before Woods could think of anything to say, Monyane touched Richie's shoulder. 'Tell them, one Lesotho official and seven holders of United Nations passports.'

Woods smiled and nodded to Richie to repeat the message on the radio.

For a long time they continued to fly in and out of clouds. At last, they came out into the sun and Woods knew they must be close to Botswana. Woods looked down at the country below them – hills, green farms, cattle. It would always be his country, Woods knew that, even though he knew he might never see it again. He held the pages of the manuscript in his bag. Woods knew, and Biko had believed, that men's minds could be changed; but could they be changed before the price became too high? What a cost had already been paid! The inquest had decided that Biko had died after falling down. Mapetla had 'hanged himself'. Many others had died in custody, trying to change South Africa.

'Dad . . . look! A city!' Duncan called.

Woods looked out of the window. 'Yes, that's it. Across the river. We are safe . . .'

And his eyes turned back to that beautiful land of his birth. In his mind he heard the crowd of thousands singing at Biko's funeral.

God bless Africa,
Raise up her name,
Hear our prayers
And bless us . . .

Bless the leaders,
Bless also the young
That they may carry the
    land with patience,
In their youth, bless them.

Bless our efforts
To work together and lift
    ourselves
Through learning and
    understanding,
God bless us.

Woza Moya! Yihla Moya!
Come, Spirit! Descend, Spirit!
Woza Moya Oyingcwele!
Come, Holy Spirit!

And the plane turned its nose down to land.

GLOSSARY

acacia a small tree with white or yellow flowers

Acting *(adj)* temporarily doing the job of another person

Afrikaans a South African language developed from 17th-century Dutch

Afrikaner a South African, descended from the Dutch, who speaks Afrikaans

Amen a word used to show sincere approval of something that has just been said (used, for example, at the end of a prayer)

authority the power to give orders to other people and make them obey

ban *(v)* to forbid someone by law from doing or saying something

banning area the area where, by law, a banned person must stay

Bantu a word used by white South Africans for black people (Biko's first name was Bantu, his full name being Bantu Stephen Biko)

Black Consciousness a South African organization, led by Stephen Biko, which believed that black people should achieve success without the help of white people

bless *(v)* to ask God for protection

bug *(v)* to hide a small machine in a room or a telephone in order to listen secretly to private conversations

bulldozer a powerful tractor with a large steel blade at the front, which can move earth or destroy buildings

charges accusations of a crime which will be brought to court

clinic a place where people see doctors for treatment or advice

coffin a box for a dead person to be buried in

concentration camp a prison for political prisoners or prisoners of war

confrontation face-to-face challenge of ideas and forces

custody in prison, waiting for trial

dye *(n)* a liquid used to change the colour of things; **dye** *(v)*

editor the person who is in charge of a newspaper

editorial a special article in a newspaper, usually written by the editor

High Commission the office of a group of people who represent the government of a foreign country

hitch-hike to travel by getting free rides in other people's cars

Holy Spirit in the Christian religion, God in the form of a spirit

Homeland an area of South Africa reserved for black people to live in

hood a cover, like a bag, for the head and part of the face

inquest an official enquiry to learn the facts about a death

justice the quality or ideal of being right and fair

Land Rover a strong car designed for use over rough ground

liberal *(n)* a person who wants progress and individual freedom in society

manuscript an author's work, handwritten or typed

minder a person employed to watch someone

mortuary a building where dead bodies are kept before burial

naked without clothes on

nappy a small towel folded round a baby's bottom

newsroom the office of a newspaper where journalists work

partition a thin wall which divides a room into smaller rooms

pass *(n)* a document giving somebody permission to be in a particular area

permit *(n)* a document which allows a person to go somewhere or do something

poster a large notice or picture displayed in a public place

print *(v)* to produce a copy of a newspaper or book

publish to produce a book and offer it for sale to the public

racism believing that people of one skin colour are better than people of another skin colour

raid *(n)* a sudden attack made by the police or the army

reflex an automatic, not a conscious, movement of the body

road-block something which blocks a road so that the police can check the traffic

security (men) police whose duty is to protect the interests of the government

stadium a large sports field, surrounded by seats

stand up to (somebody) to refuse to give in; to defend oneself with courage

State Prosecutor a lawyer who speaks for the government in a law court

tear gas a gas which hurts people's eyes and produces tears, used by the police to control violent crowds

township a town in South Africa reserved for black people

tribal of a group of people with the same language, customs, beliefs, etc.

van a type of closed lorry used to carry and deliver things

warrant a document which allows the police to arrest someone or to search a house

witness box the place in a law court where a witness gives evidence

ACTIVITIES

Before Reading

1 Read the back cover and the story introduction on the first page of the book. How much do you know now about this story? For each sentence, circle **Y** (yes) or **N** (no).

1 Steve Biko talked of peace and friendship. Y/N
2 Steve Biko died of hunger. Y/N
3 Before 1994, South Africa had a white government. Y/N
4 South Africa is rich in gold and diamonds. Y/N
5 Donald Woods was a political leader. Y/N
6 Steve Biko was forbidden by the government to speak freely about his ideas. Y/N
7 This book is based on a film. Y/N
8 This is a story about people who are afraid to die. Y/N

2 Which of these statements about South Africa today do you think are true? How would you rewrite those that are not true?

1 South Africa is one of the poorest countries in Africa.
2 There are many more black people than white people in South Africa.
3 Nelson Mandela became the first black president of South Africa.
4 Most black people in South Africa are now rich.
5 Most whites have left South Africa.
6 Rugby, football, and cricket are popular sports in South Africa.

ACTIVITIES

While Reading

Read Chapters 1 and 2, and then answer these questions.

1 Describe three of the photos of the police raid on Crossroads.
2 Why did the police raid the black township called Crossroads?
3 Describe what Donald Woods thought about black people.
4 Why did Mamphela Ramphele want Woods to go and see Steve Biko?
5 Describe what was happening in the church centre when Woods went in.
6 What did blacks use the word 'System' to describe?
7 What was the idea that made Biko laugh aloud?

Read Chapters 3 to 5. Choose the best question-word for these questions, and then answer them.

What / Who / Why / Where

1 ... sort of organizations did Woods believe that South Africa needed?
2 ... was the question Biko asked that embarrassed Woods?
3 ... did the money for the clinic at Zanempilo come from?
4 ... didn't Mamphela want Biko to go to the township with Woods?
5 ... work did most of the women in the township do?
6 ... owned the land in South Africa?
7 ... didn't Biko and his friends approve of the aims of white liberals?
8 ... did Tenjy believe black society could teach other societies?

Read Chapters 6 to 9. Who said this, and to whom? Who or what were they talking about?

1 '. . . the Board has approved their appointment here.'
2 'Last year they killed more than four hundred black students!'
3 'No, man, don't beat him!'
4 'You and I are now in confrontation, but I see no violence.'
5 '. . . he told you himself that he wants to fight police illegality.'
6 '. . . he is a black leader you can talk to.'
7 'Do you think we are going to give all this away?'
8 'The next time he sends you, you had better bring a warrant.'
9 'They think I'm at the clinic.'
10 'Bring it to the window over there and I'll read it.'

Read Chapters 10 and 11. How did the 'System' fight back? Correct the mistakes in this very inaccurate report.

Mapetla was the first to be arrested. Tenjy was arrested next, on charges of terrorism, and a week later Mapetla died at home. The police said he had shot himself, and Woods knew this was true. At the inquest Biko said the bruises on Mapetla's neck were caused by a rugby injury. The police were blamed for Mapetla's death. Then Biko was arrested because he hit a policeman. The doctor who saw Biko in prison found him conscious but slightly injured. The police sent Biko in an ambulance to the nearest hospital.

Read Chapters 12 to 14, and then answer these questions.

1 What happened in the black townships after Biko's death?
2 Why did the sight of Biko's face shock Woods?
3 Why did Woods hesitate when invited to Biko's funeral?
4 What emotions were expressed by the crowd at Biko's funeral?

5 Why did Woods want to go to America after Biko's death?

6 What four things was Woods forbidden to do for five years?

7 How did Woods learn that his house was bugged?

8 What were Woods' reasons for wanting to publish his book?

9 Why did Wendy change her mind about leaving the country?

Before you read the rest of the story, can you guess the answers to these questions?

1 How does Woods escape – by car, plane, boat, or on foot?

2 Can he escape from the country without anybody's help?

3 Do his family travel with him, or join him later, or stay behind in South Africa?

Read Chapters 15 to 18, and then answer these questions.

1 How did Woods disguise himself?

2 Why was 31st December a good date to escape?

3 Why couldn't the Woods family say goodbye to each other?

4 How did Woods escape from his own house?

5 Why was Woods unable to walk across the river into Lesotho?

6 How did Woods get to Telle Bridge?

7 Why did the official say that Woods was a brave man?

8 When Wendy and the children left the house, where did the watching policeman think they were going?

9 Why was Woods in such a hurry to get to a phone?

10 Why was Wendy afraid to talk to Woods on the phone?

11 Why was it dangerous for the Woods family to fly out of Lesotho?

12 How did Chief Jonathan show his support for Woods?

ACTIVITIES

After Reading

1 **After Donald went to the black township with Biko, perhaps he wrote his diary. Choose one suitable word to fill each gap.**

Biko was right. Black people know _____ we whites live, but we have _____ idea how black South Africans live. _____ we went to the township, there _____ nine of us in the taxi. _____ sat in the back, wearing somebody's _____ to cover my hair. I was _____ squashed that I couldn't even move _____ hands. We drove around, watching the _____ of people until the evening rush _____ over. Then four of us went _____ foot down the side streets. The _____ is full of violence. Gangs of _____ walk the streets. Most women work _____ domestic servants, so they see their _____ only on Sundays. Biko took me _____ eat with a black family – twelve _____ living in four rooms, with no _____, and they have to fetch water _____ an outside tap and heat it _____ the cooker. We sat and talked _____ the differences between black and white _____, and I tried to understand their _____ and their bitterness. I realize now _____ I have never understood the feelings _____ the black community.

2 **Imagine that Biko told Woods about the night the police came to his house (in Chapter 9). Complete their conversation.**

WOODS: Hello, Steve. Did you finish that article last night?
BIKO: _____
WOODS: Why not? What happened?
BIKO: _____

WOODS: Were you expecting anybody?

BIKO: _____

WOODS: And then?

BIKO: _____

WOODS: It was the police, I suppose.

BIKO: Yes. Lemick, and my two regular minders.

WOODS: _____

BIKO: He said he had orders to search my house for dangerous documents.

WOODS: _____

BIKO: Yes, he did. So I asked him to bring it to the window so that I could read it.

WOODS: But what did you do with the papers?

BIKO: _____

WOODS: Very clever! And did they search the house?

BIKO: _____

3 **Complete this passage about Biko's ideas with the words below (one word for each gap).**

challenge, confront, confrontation, force, humanity, influence, terrorism, terrorists, violence, violent

The government often accused black leaders of being _____, but Biko thought the government itself was guilty of _____. He wanted black people to _____ the problems of society and to build a sense of their own _____. But although he called for direct _____, he meant a face-to-face _____ of ideas, not _____ action. He did not believe that _____ was the solution and he wanted to _____ the government by the _____ of his arguments.

4 **Do you agree (A) or disagree (D) with these statements about Chapter 11? Explain why.**

1 The security police were doing what the government wanted, so they were not to blame for Biko's injuries.

2 The police did not realize how serious Biko's injuries were, and that the drive to Pretoria would almost certainly kill him.

3 The doctor should have demanded that Biko was taken to the nearest hospital, even at personal risk to himself.

4 The police and the doctor were equally responsible for Biko's death.

5 Fear is a more powerful emotion than love.

5 **After Biko's funeral, Wendy writes a letter to her mother. Use these notes to write the letter for her.**

Arrived at the stadium early. Large crowd. Posters. Government and church officials on the platform. Some whites. Processions arrived. Singing. Coffin, flowers. Speaker talked of road-blocks, then of hope for South Africa. Emotions of crowd. Song of Africa – Donald sings in English for white students.

6 **Put this summary of how Woods crossed the border into Lesotho in the right order. Then, using these linking words, join the parts together to make a paragraph of five sentences.**

after / and / and / and although / and when / but / that / then / what

1 _____ the driver offered him a lift across the bridge

2 _____ was in his bag

3 suddenly a Land Rover came down the hill very fast

4 _____ Woods had waved goodbye to Tami
5 Woods saw with relief
6 _____ Woods saw ahead of him the wet green hills of Lesotho
7 no questions were asked about Woods' passport
8 _____ stopped right in front of him
9 he walked to the iron gate at the start of the bridge
10 crossing the frontier out of South Africa
11 _____ it was locked and there was no one around
12 he did not ask him to open it
13 he accepted gratefully
14 _____ it was the postal service, and not the police
15 _____ a frontier policeman asked Woods
16 _____ Moses drove slowly across the bridge

7 **Which of these statements about *Cry Freedom* do you agree (A) with, and which you do disagree (D) with? Explain why.**

1 Woods changed his views on South African society because of his friendship with Biko.
2 Woods was right to employ Tenjy and Mapetla at the *Daily Dispatch*.
3 Woods should have told Kruger the name of the witness who saw the police smash the community centre.
4 Biko should not have gone to the meeting of black students in Cape Town.
5 Biko should have taken fewer risks because of his family.
6 Woods was right to print the pictures of Biko's body.
7 Woods was selfish to ask Wendy to leave South Africa.
8 Biko's death probably helped to change the political situation in South Africa.

ABOUT THE BOOK, THE FILM, AND SOUTH AFRICA

John Briley was born in Kalamazoo, Michigan, in the USA. He is best known as a screenwriter, but he has also written several novels. In all, Briley has written fifteen screenplays, including *Children of the Damned* (1965). He won an Oscar for the screenplay for *Gandhi* (1983), which was produced and directed by Richard Attenborough.

In 1987 he wrote the screenplay for *Cry Freedom* (also produced and directed by Richard Attenborough). The film starred Denzel Washington as Stephen Biko and Kevin Kline as Donald Woods, and was shot in Zimbabwe. The film was based on two factual books written by the South African journalist Donald Woods after he escaped from South Africa – *Biko* (1978), and *Asking for Trouble: The Autobiography of a Banned Journalist* (1980). The film *Cry Freedom* was so popular that John Briley wrote a novel based on the screenplay.

Donald Woods has said that the film *Cry Freedom* gives a truthful account of what really happened. Some things that happened were left out of the film because they might have seemed exaggerated. For example, when Biko hit the policeman who was questioning him, there were actually seven security policemen in the cell.

Donald Woods, after living in exile in London for many years, is now able to return regularly to South Africa where he is involved in training black journalists as part of a project called the Steve Biko Memorial Bursary.

In 1997, the Truth and Reconciliation Commission in South Africa questioned five security policemen who were involved in Biko's death. They admitted hitting him and chaining him to the security bars of his cell for twenty-four hours. Peter Jones, who was arrested with Biko in 1977 and who survived eighteen months in prison, spoke on behalf of Biko's family. On the twentieth anniversary of Biko's death, on 12th September 1997, there was a national celebration in South Africa. Thousands came to the East London City Hall to watch President Nelson Mandela unveil a statue of Biko. The main bridge over the Buffalo river in East London has been renamed the Steve Biko bridge. Steve Biko has not been forgotten.

OXFORD BOOKWORMS LIBRARY

Classics • Crime & Mystery • Factfiles • Fantasy & Horror
Human Interest • Playscripts • Thriller & Adventure
True Stories • World Stories

The OXFORD BOOKWORMS LIBRARY provides enjoyable reading in English, with a wide range of classic and modern fiction, non-fiction, and plays. It includes original and adapted texts in seven carefully graded language stages, which take learners from beginner to advanced level. An overview is given on the next pages.

All Stage 1 titles are available as audio recordings, as well as over eighty other titles from Starter to Stage 6. All Starters and many titles at Stages 1 to 4 are specially recommended for younger learners. Every Bookworm is illustrated, and Starters and Factfiles have full-colour illustrations.

The OXFORD BOOKWORMS LIBRARY also offers extensive support. Each book contains an introduction to the story, notes about the author, a glossary, and activities. Additional resources include tests and worksheets, and answers for these and for the activities in the books. There is advice on running a class library, using audio recordings, and the many ways of using Oxford Bookworms in reading programmes. Resource materials are available on the website <www.oup.com/elt/gradedreaders>.

The *Oxford Bookworms Collection* is a series for advanced learners. It consists of volumes of short stories by well-known authors, both classic and modern. Texts are not abridged or adapted in any way, but carefully selected to be accessible to the advanced student.

You can find details and a full list of titles in the *Oxford Bookworms Library Catalogue* and *Oxford English Language Teaching Catalogues*, and on the website <www.oup.com/elt/gradedreaders>.

THE OXFORD BOOKWORMS LIBRARY
GRADING AND SAMPLE EXTRACTS

STARTER • 250 HEADWORDS

present simple – present continuous – imperative –
can/cannot, must – *going to* (future) – simple gerunds ...

Her phone is ringing – but where is it?

Sally gets out of bed and looks in her bag. No phone. She looks under the bed. No phone. Then she looks behind the door. There is her phone. Sally picks up her phone and answers it. *Sally's Phone*

STAGE 1 • 400 HEADWORDS

... past simple – coordination with *and, but, or* –
subordination with *before, after, when, because, so* ...

I knew him in Persia. He was a famous builder and I worked with him there. For a time I was his friend, but not for long. When he came to Paris, I came after him – I wanted to watch him. He was a very clever, very dangerous man. *The Phantom of the Opera*

STAGE 2 • 700 HEADWORDS

... present perfect – *will* (future) – *(don't) have to, must not, could* –
comparison of adjectives – simple *if* clauses – past continuous –
tag questions – *ask/tell* + infinitive ...

While I was writing these words in my diary, I decided what to do. I must try to escape. I shall try to get down the wall outside. The window is high above the ground, but I have to try. I shall take some of the gold with me – if I escape, perhaps it will be helpful later. *Dracula*

STAGE 3 • 1000 HEADWORDS

… should, may – present perfect continuous – *used to* – past perfect –
causative – relative clauses – indirect statements …

Of course, it was most important that no one should see
Colin, Mary, or Dickon entering the secret garden. So Colin
gave orders to the gardeners that they must all keep away
from that part of the garden in future. *The Secret Garden*

STAGE 4 • 1400 HEADWORDS

… past perfect continuous – passive (simple forms) –
would conditional clauses – indirect questions –
relatives with *where/when* – gerunds after prepositions/phrases …

I was glad. Now Hyde could not show his face to the world
again. If he did, every honest man in London would be proud
to report him to the police. *Dr Jekyll and Mr Hyde*

STAGE 5 • 1800 HEADWORDS

… future continuous – future perfect –
passive (modals, continuous forms) –
would have conditional clauses – modals + perfect infinitive …

If he had spoken Estella's name, I would have hit him. I was so
angry with him, and so depressed about my future, that I could
not eat the breakfast. Instead I went straight to the old house.
Great Expectations

STAGE 6 • 2500 HEADWORDS

… passive (infinitives, gerunds) – advanced modal meanings –
clauses of concession, condition

When I stepped up to the piano, I was confident. It was as if I
knew that the prodigy side of me really did exist. And when I
started to play, I was so caught up in how lovely I looked that
I didn't worry how I would sound. *The Joy Luck Club*